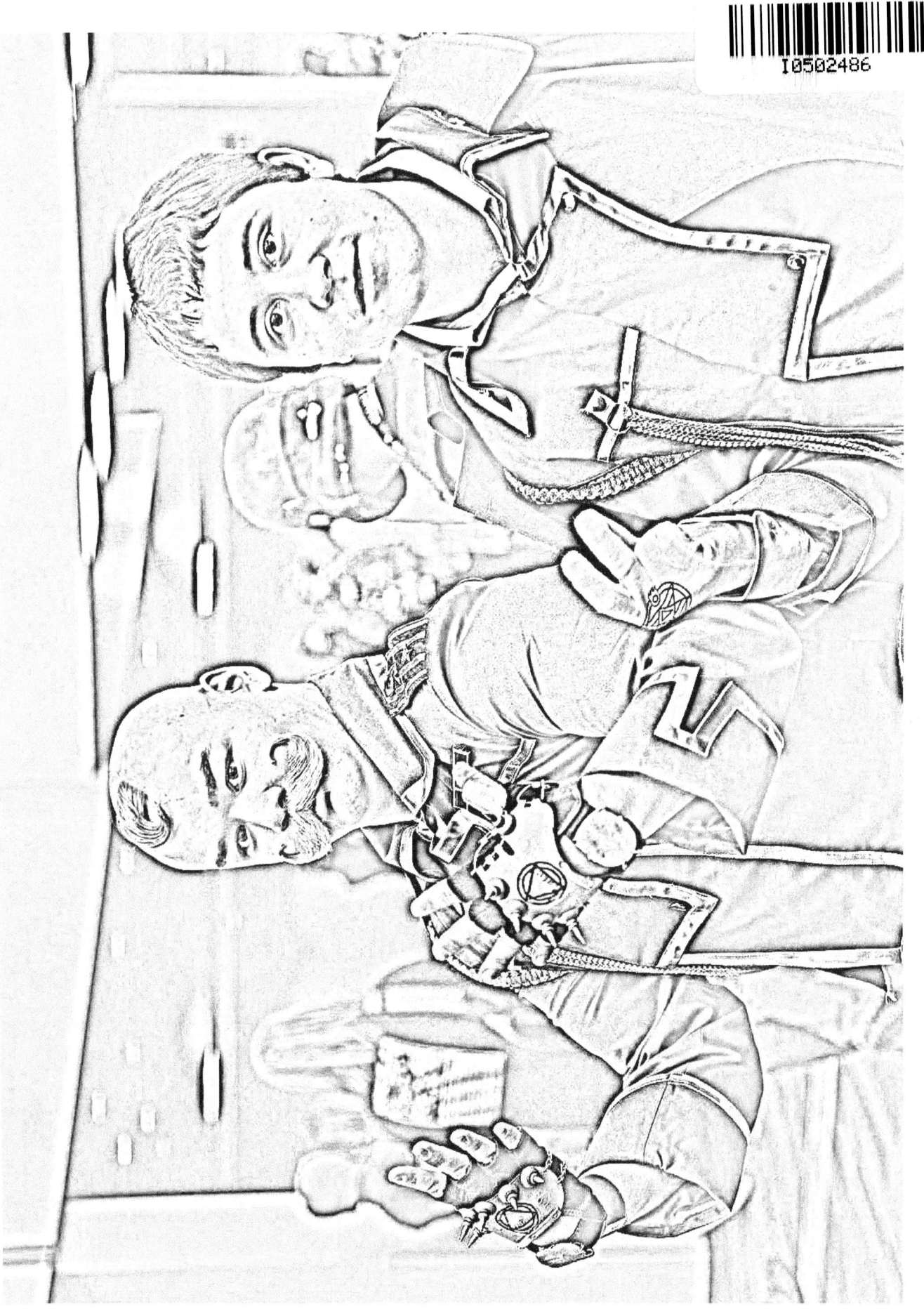

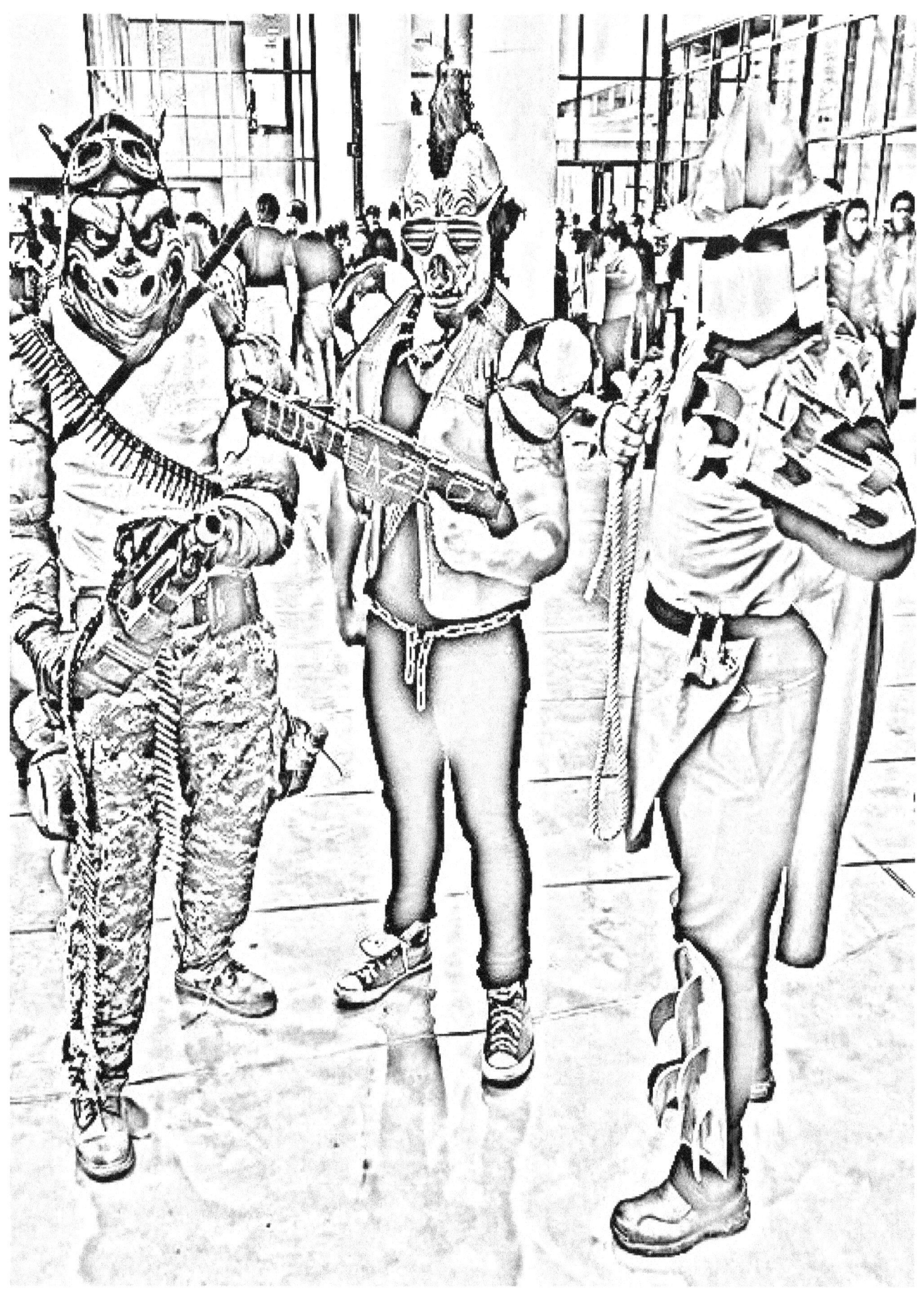

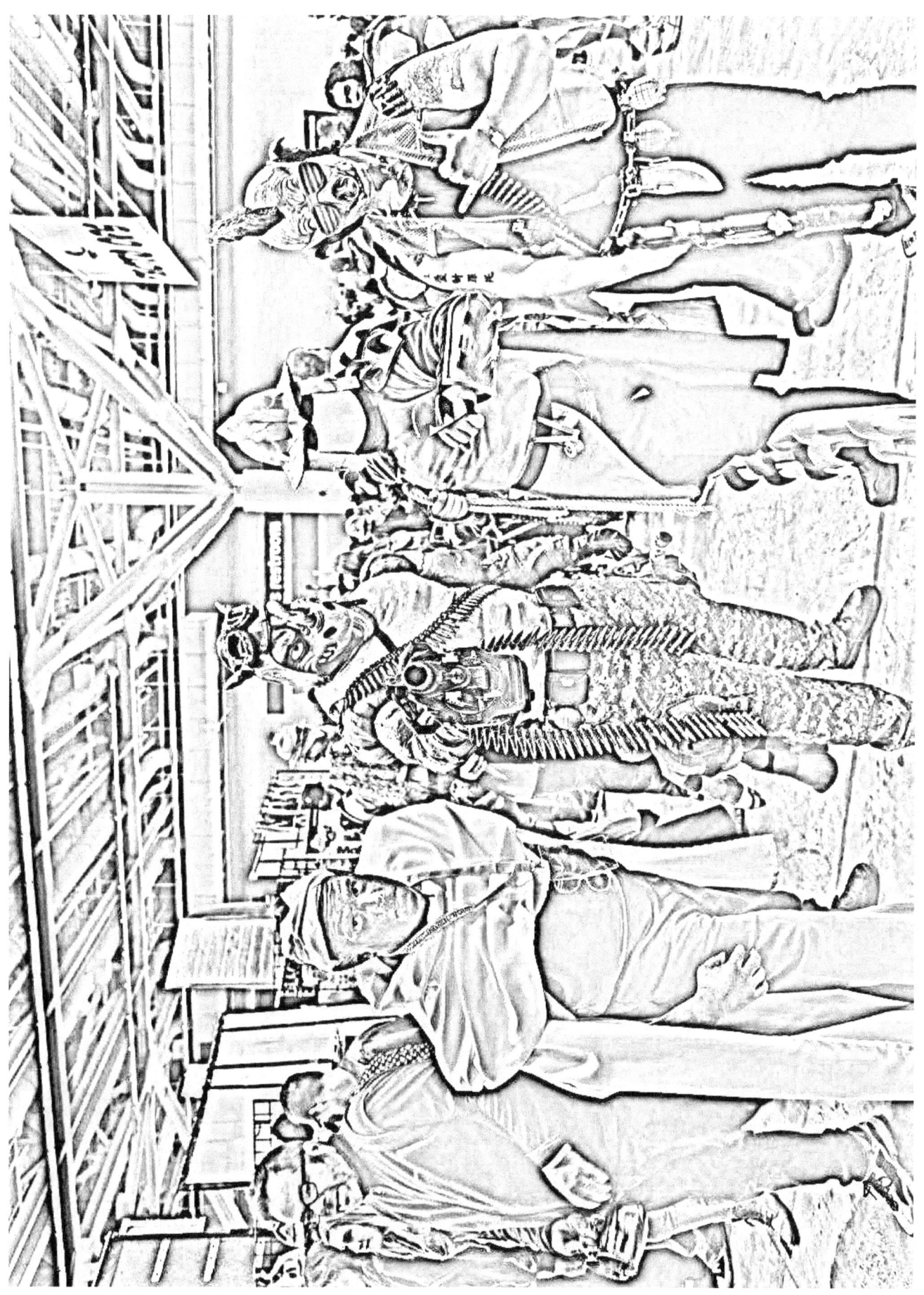

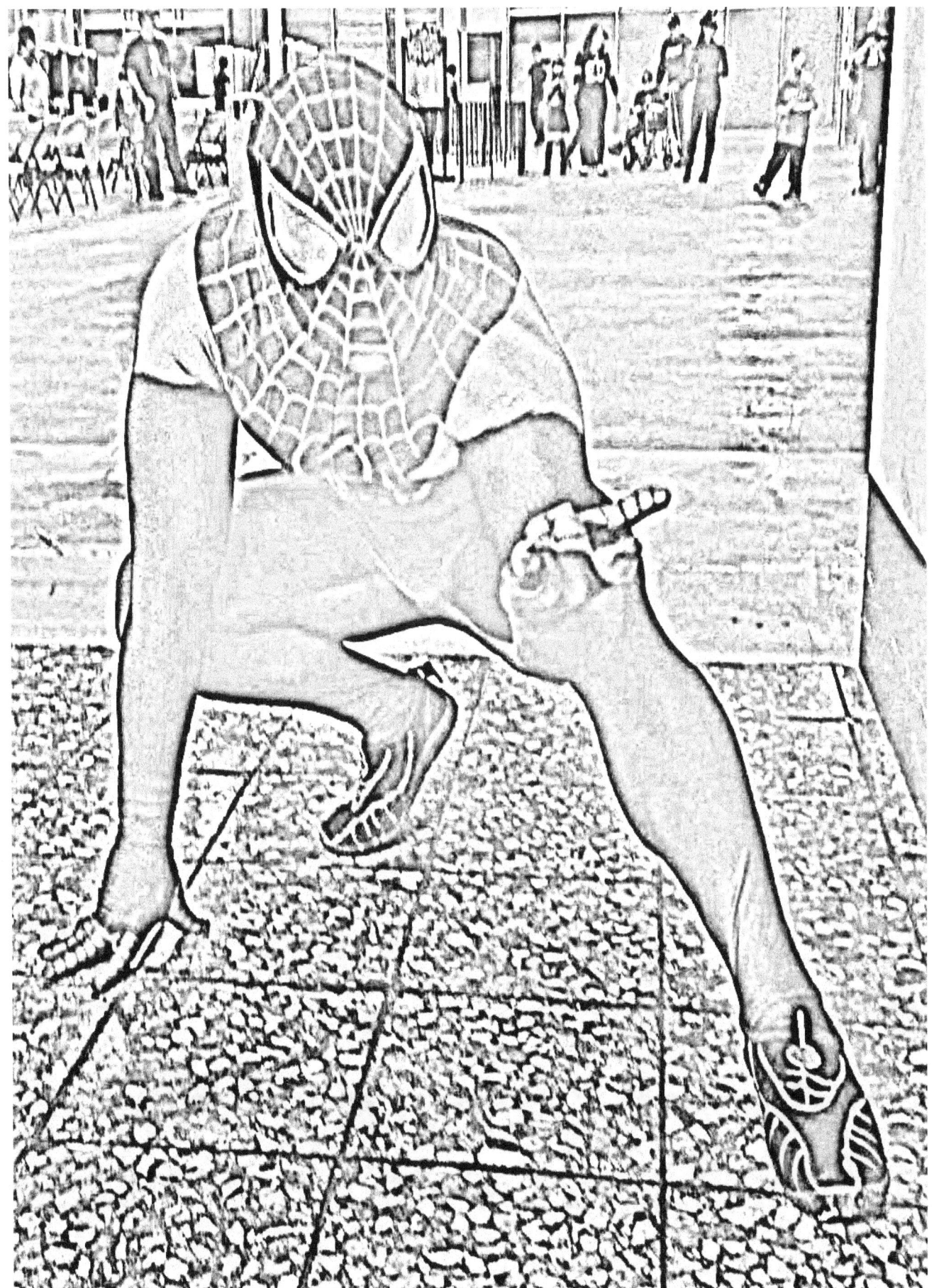

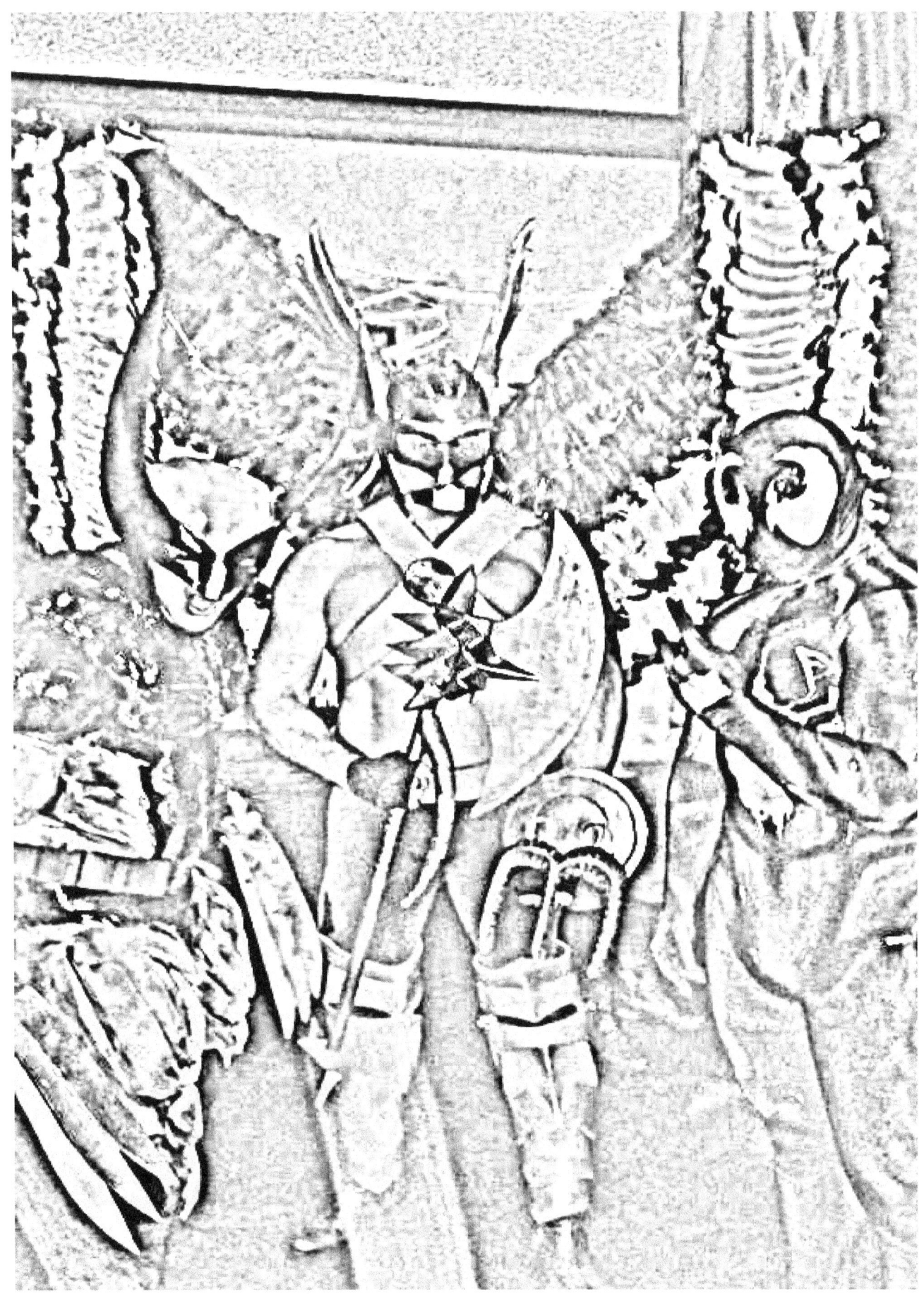

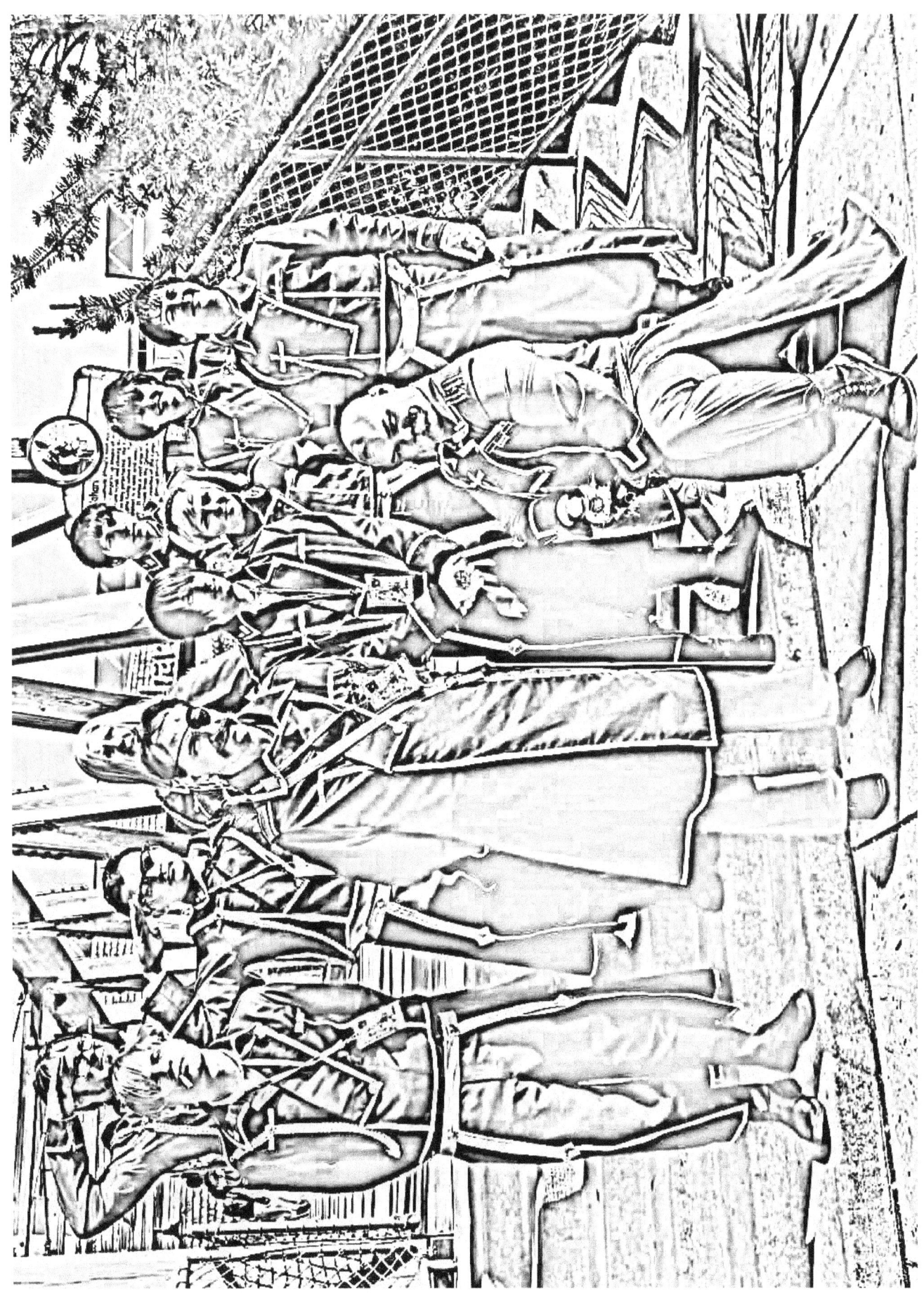

Elevator #2

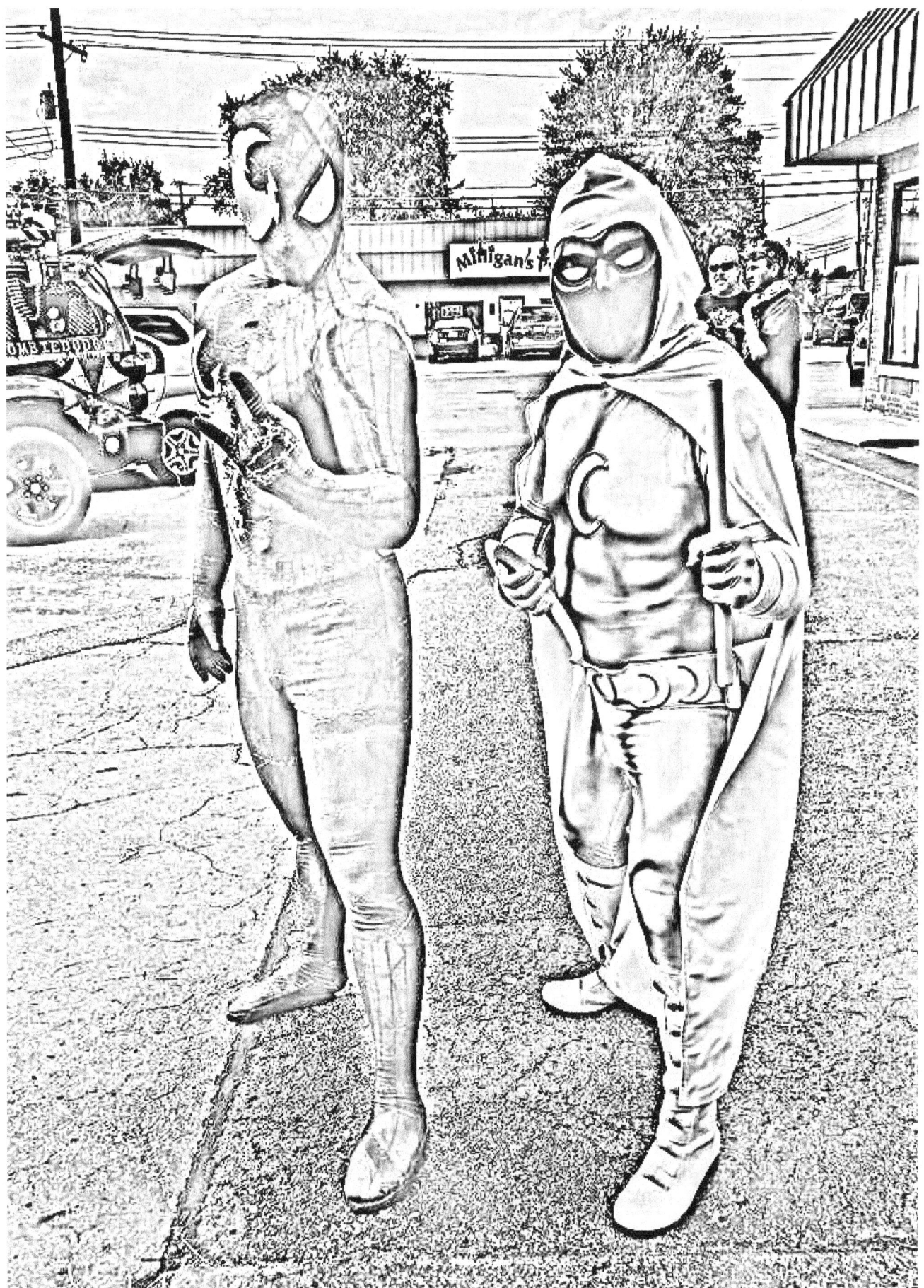

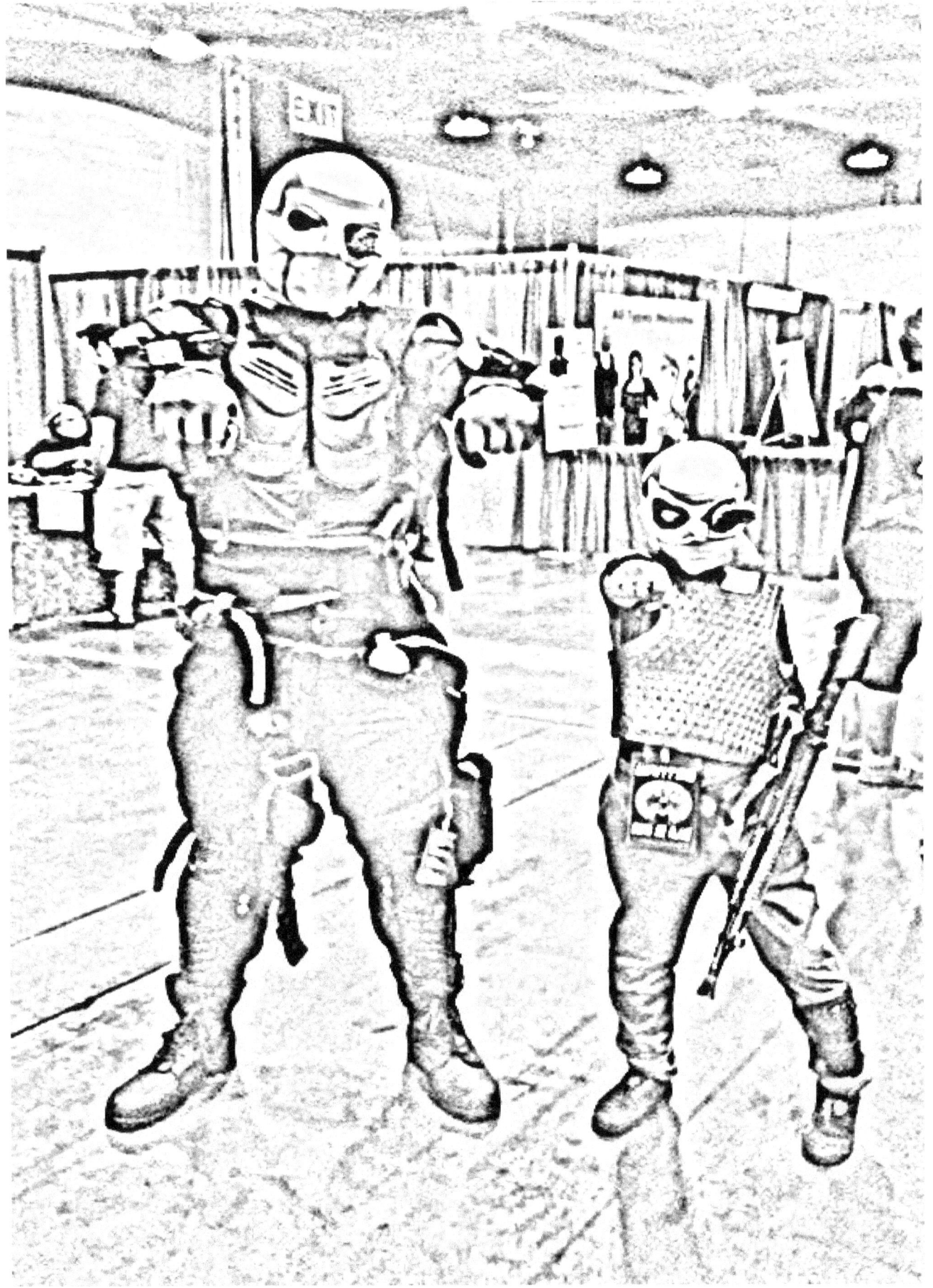

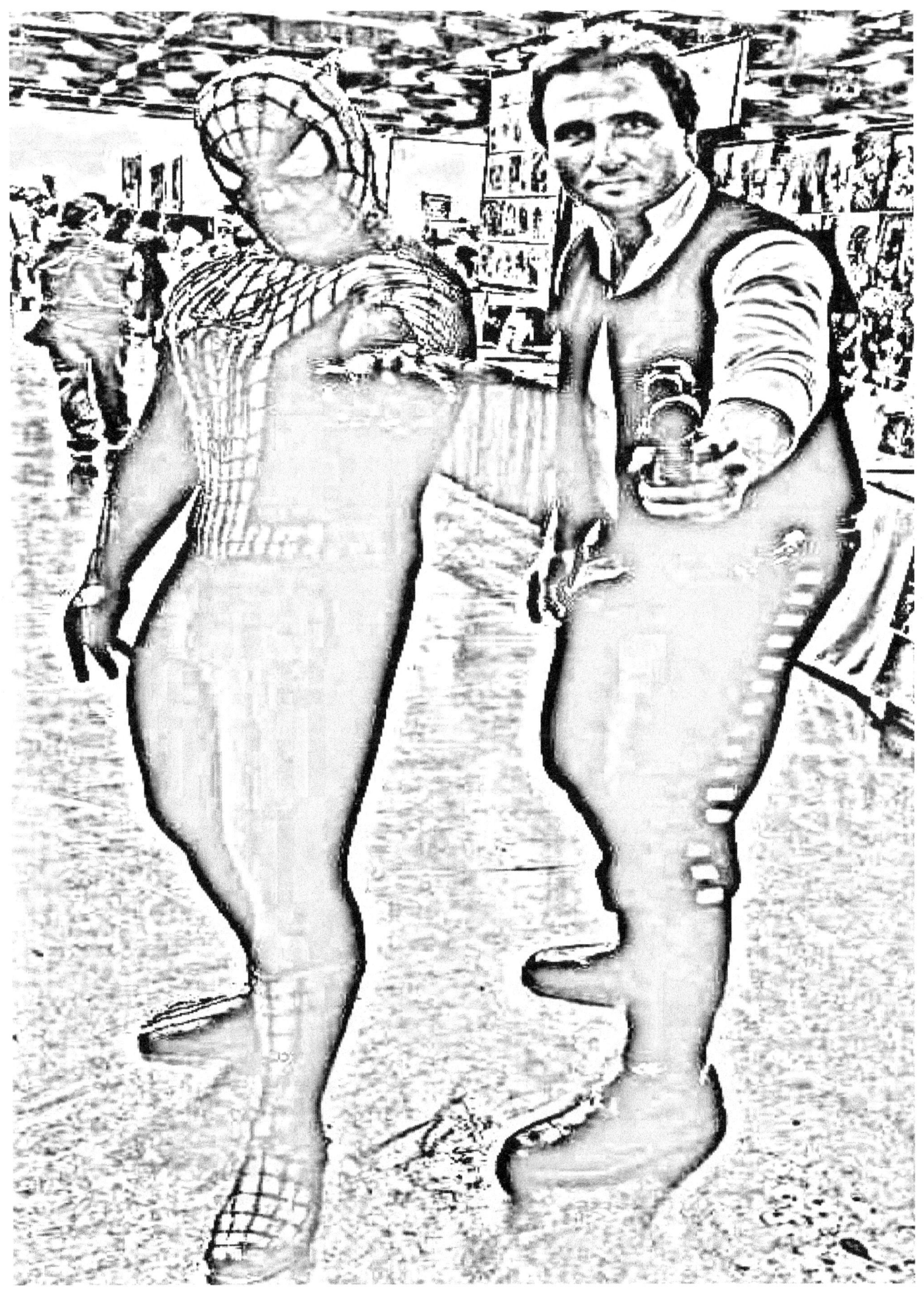

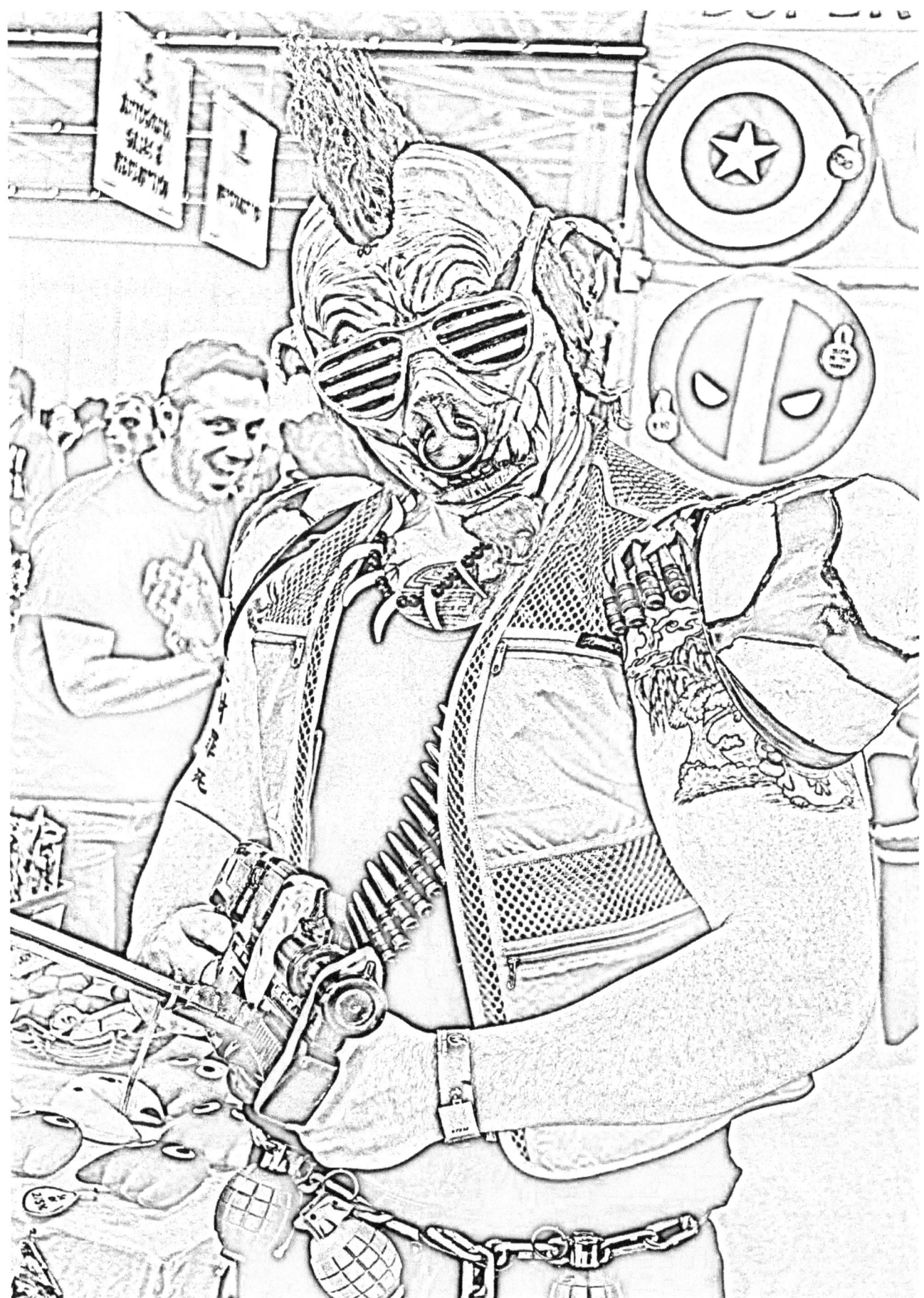

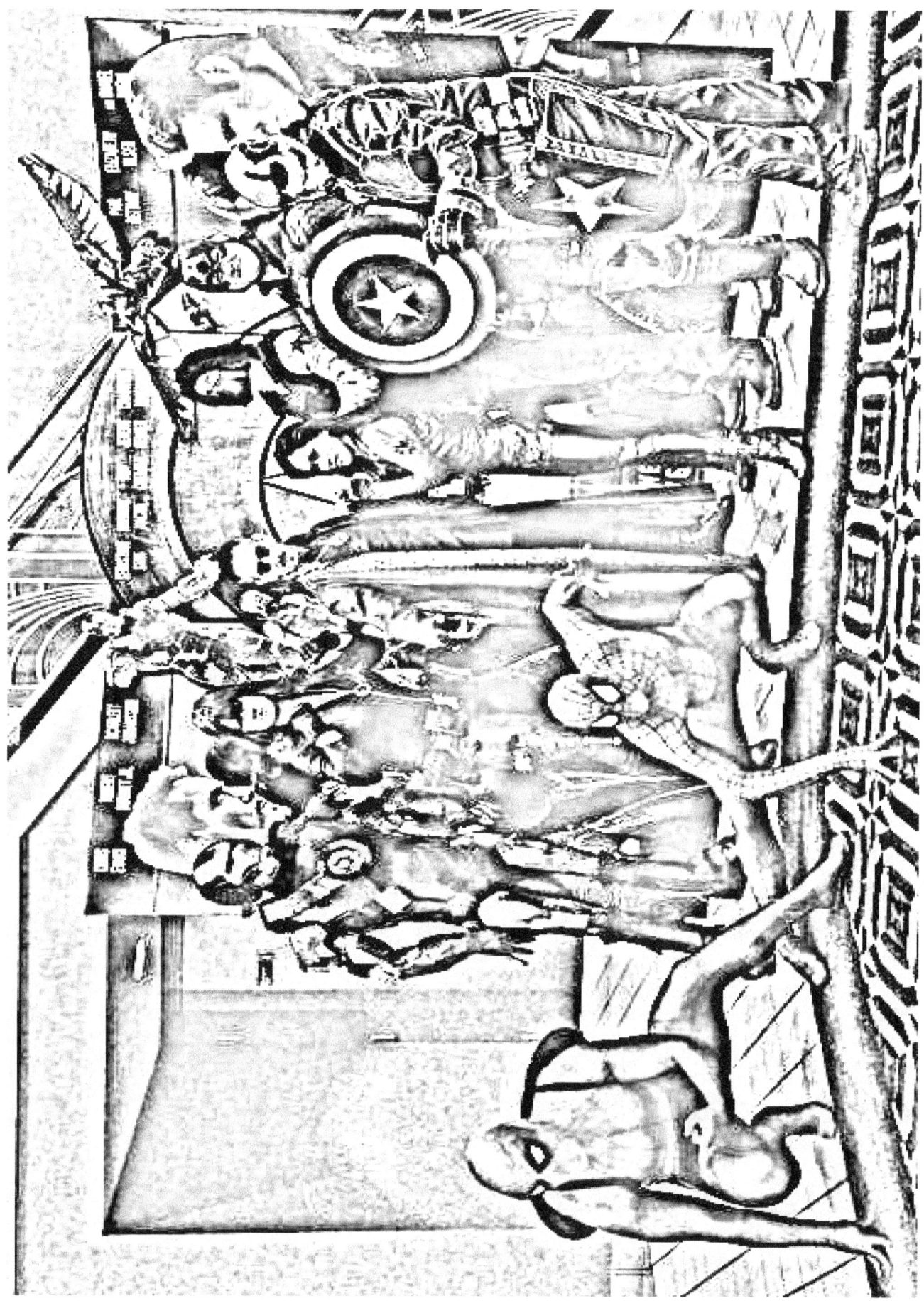

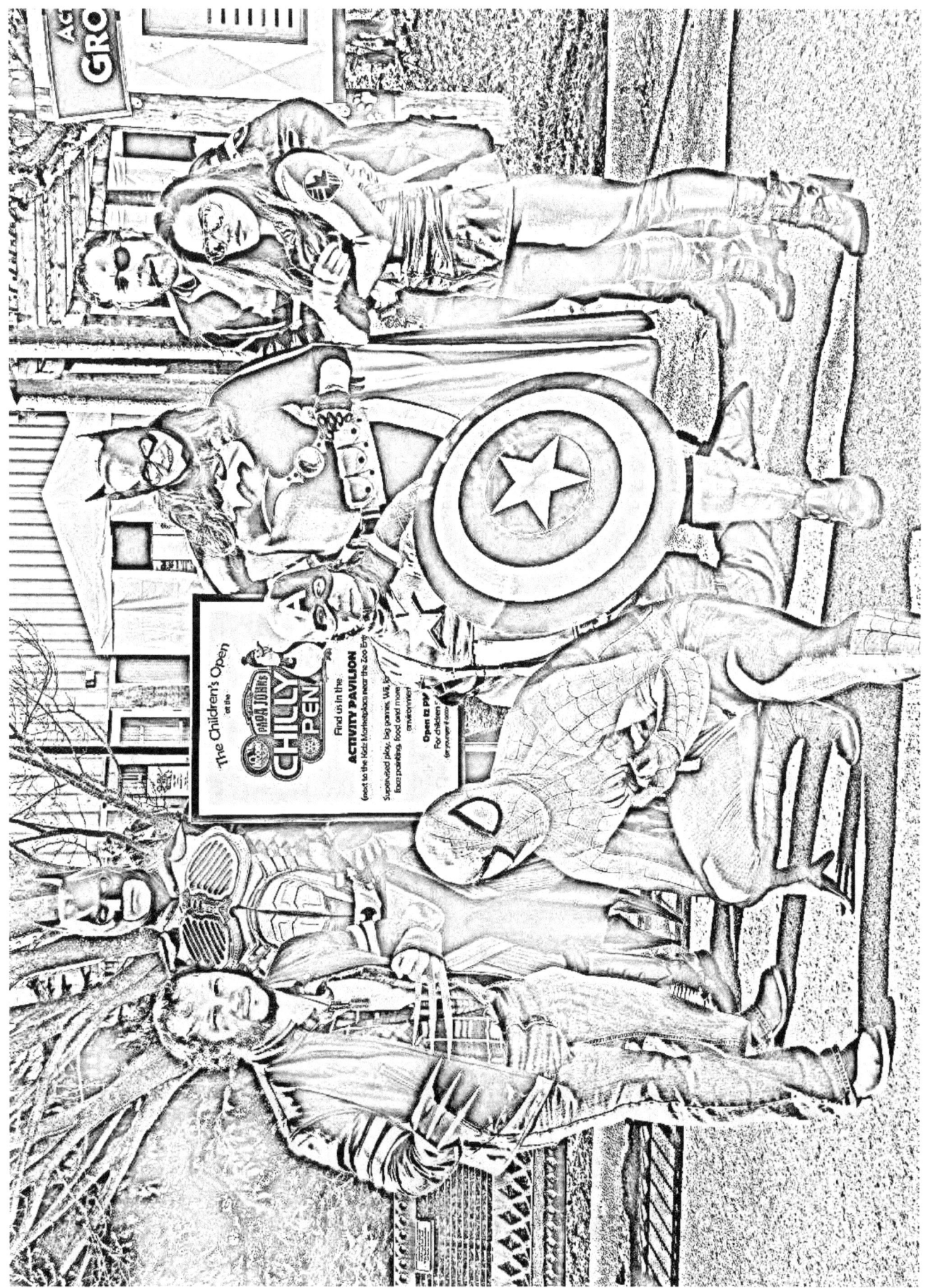

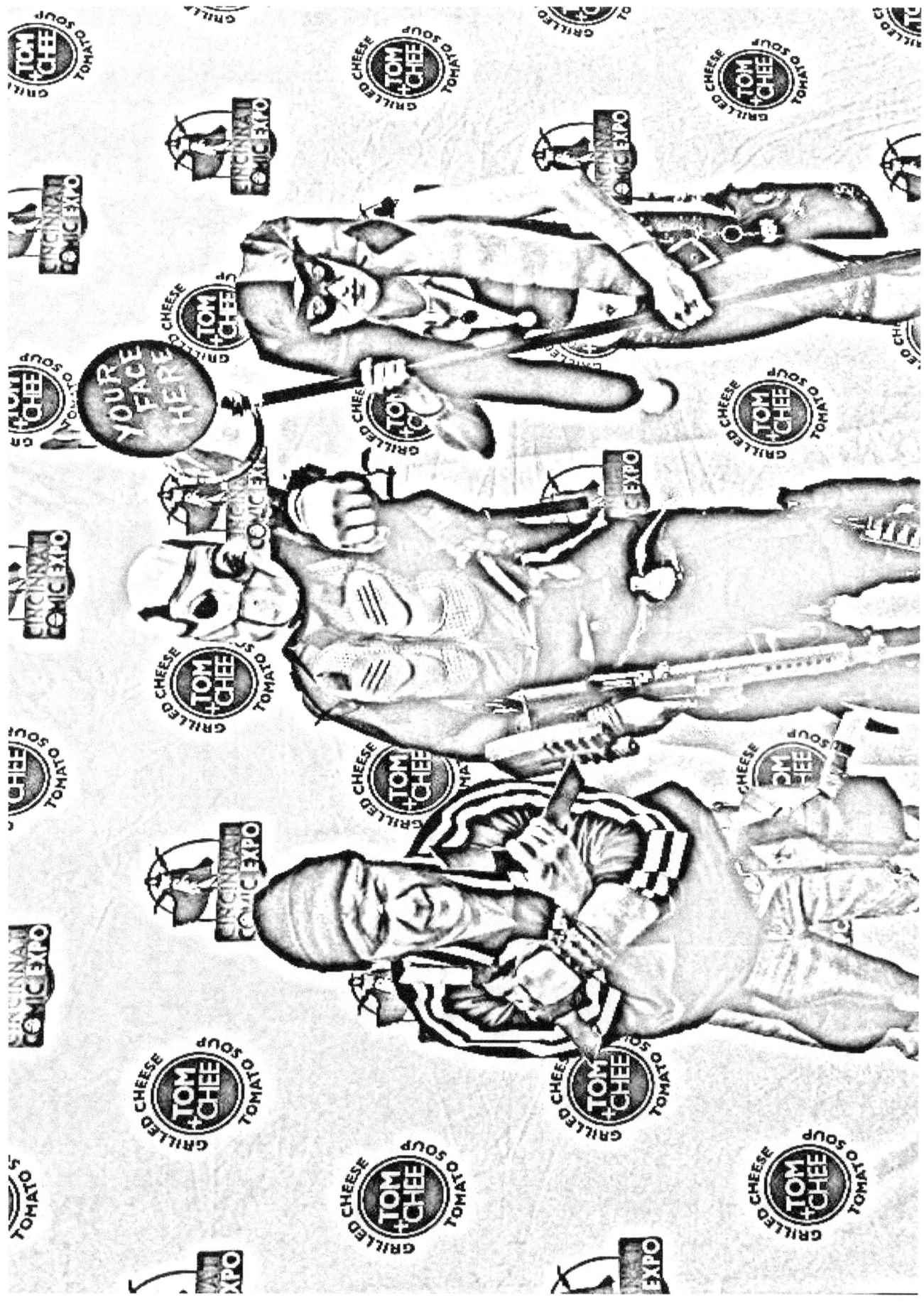

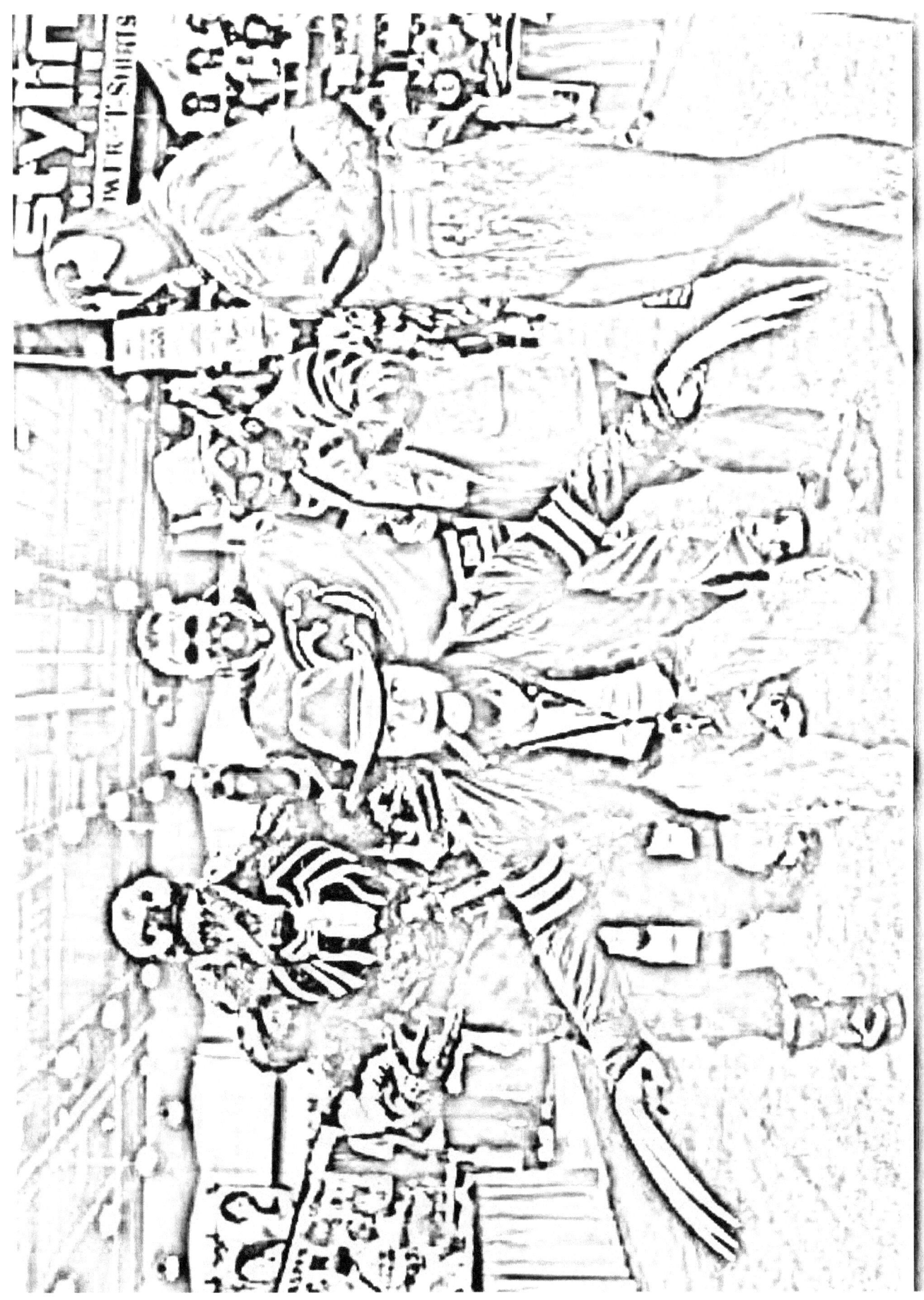

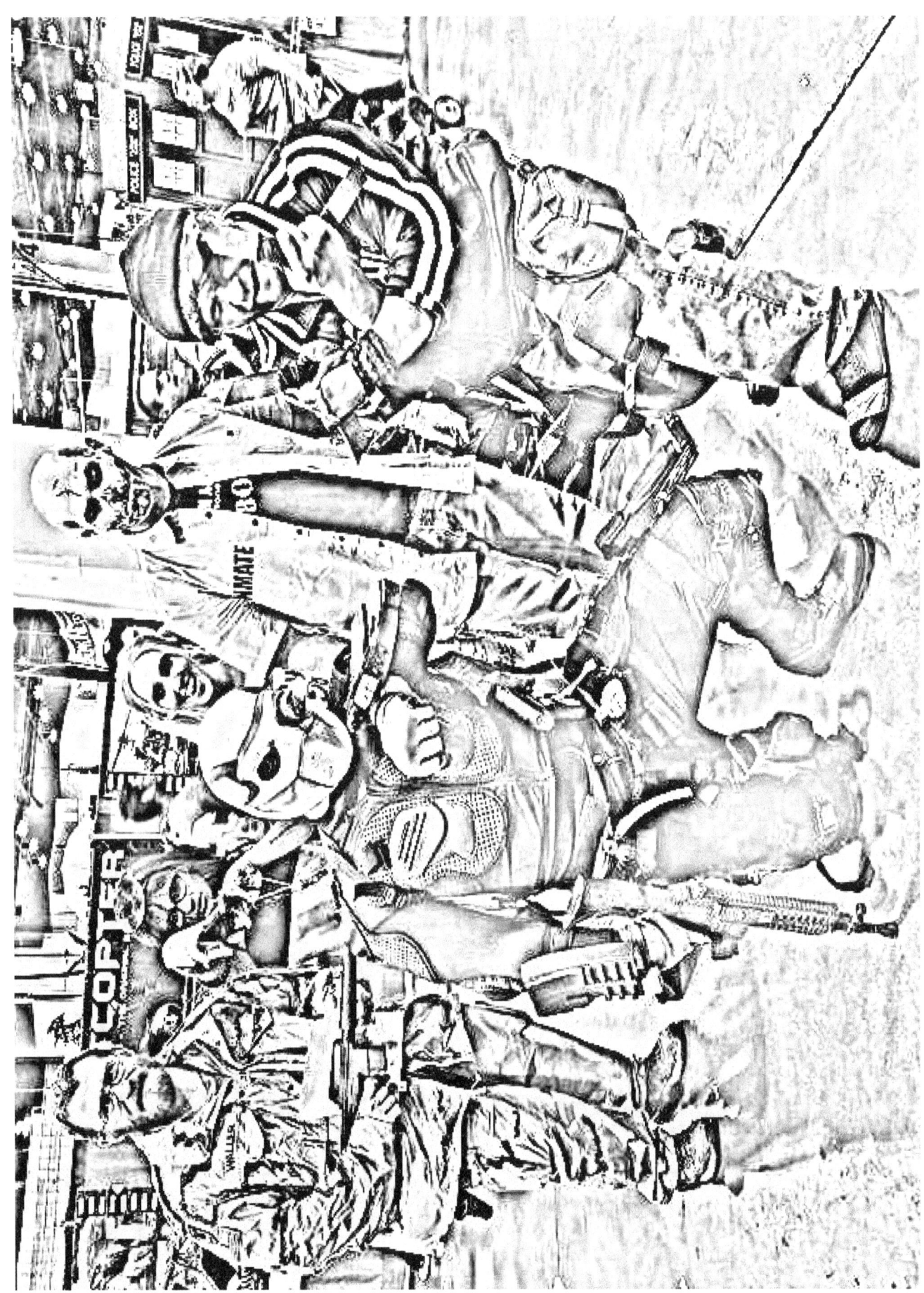

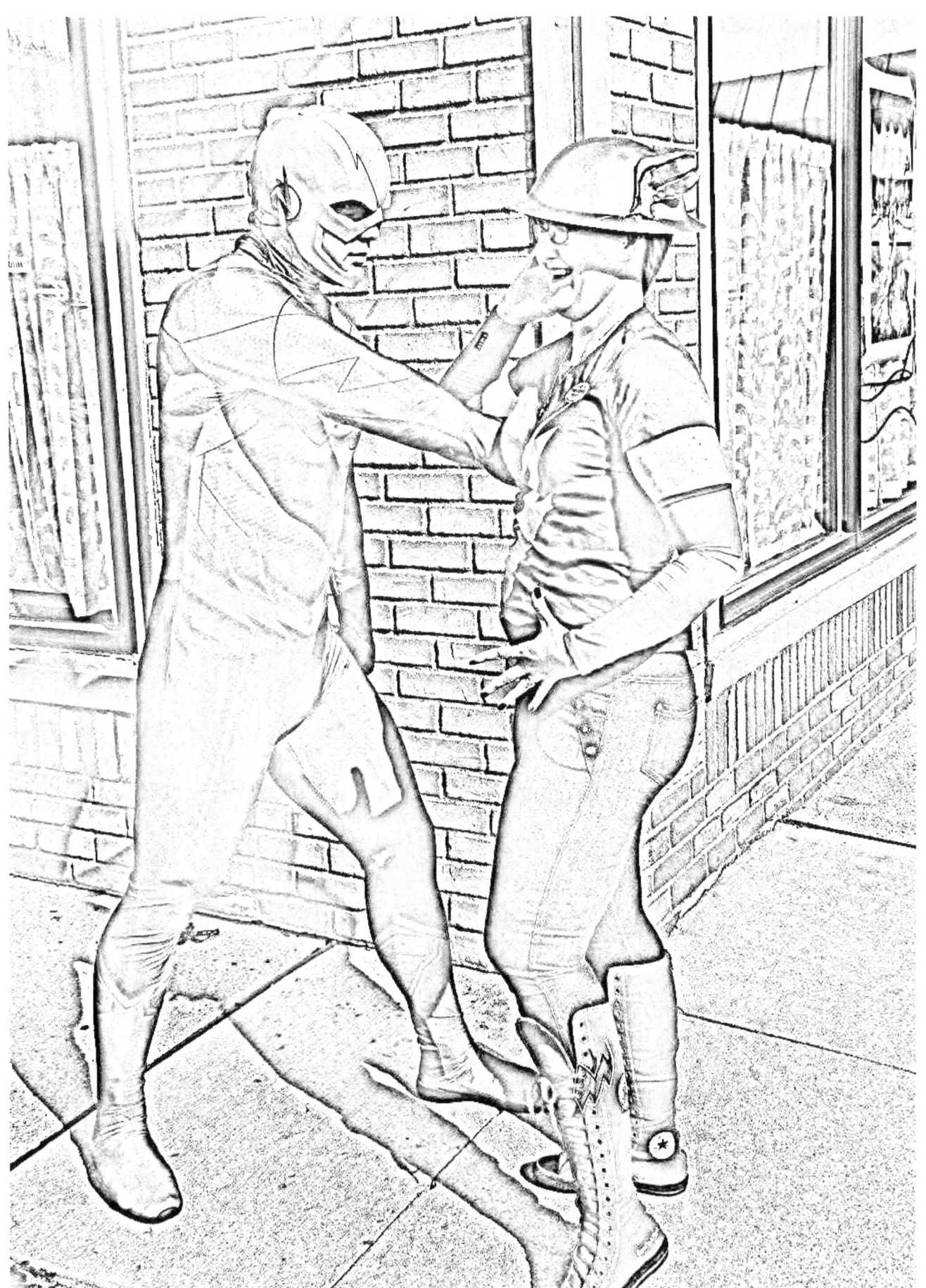

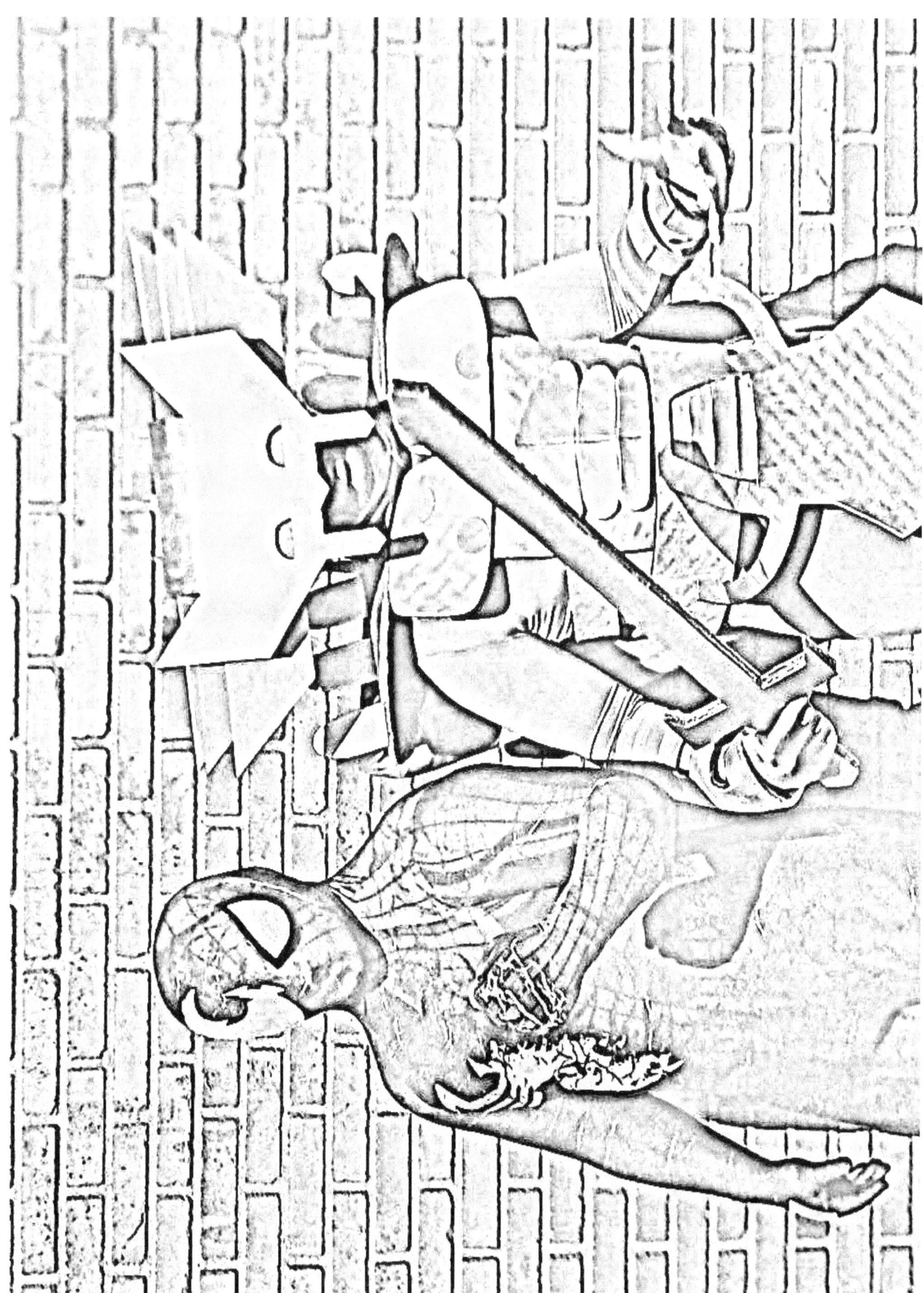

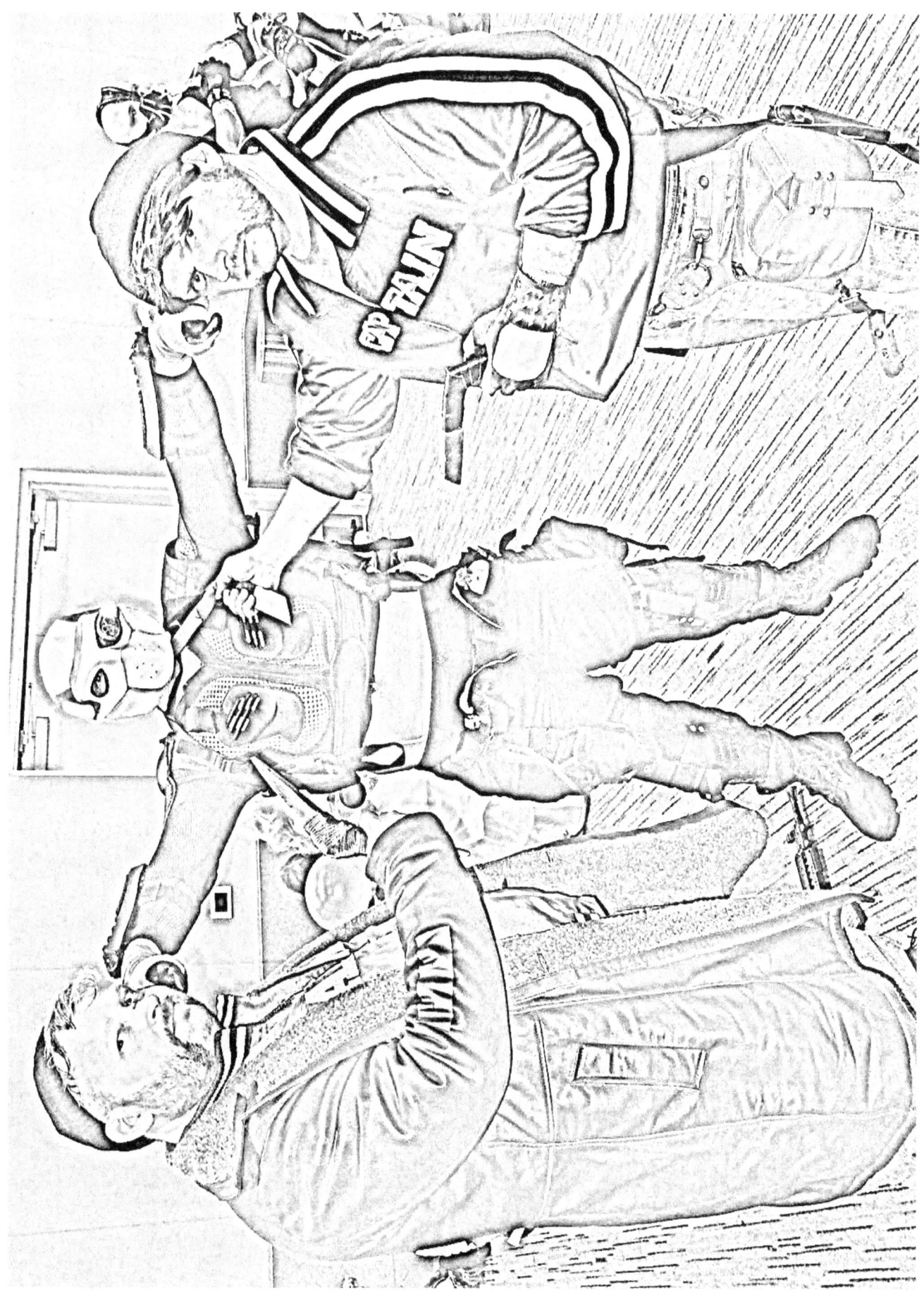

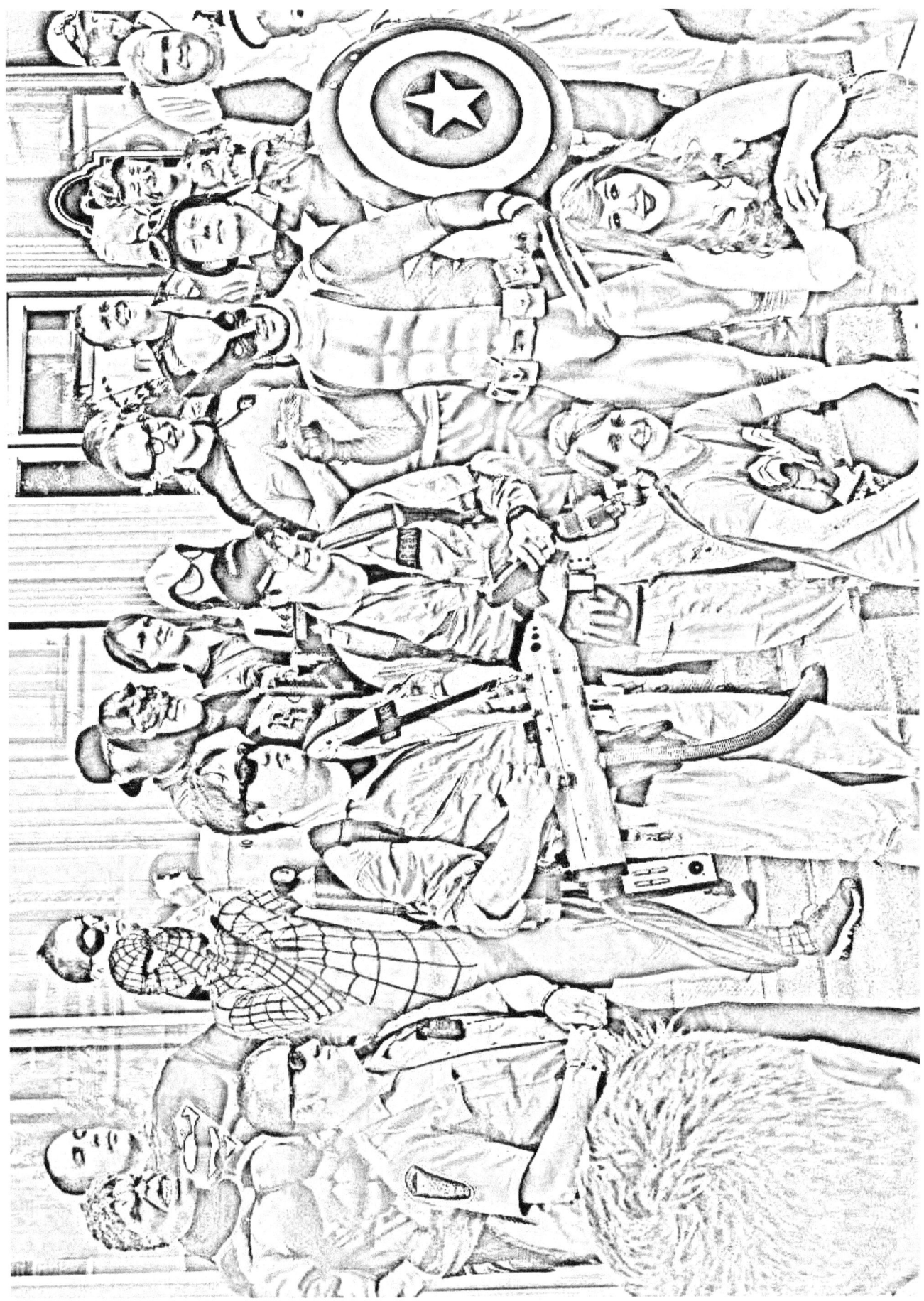

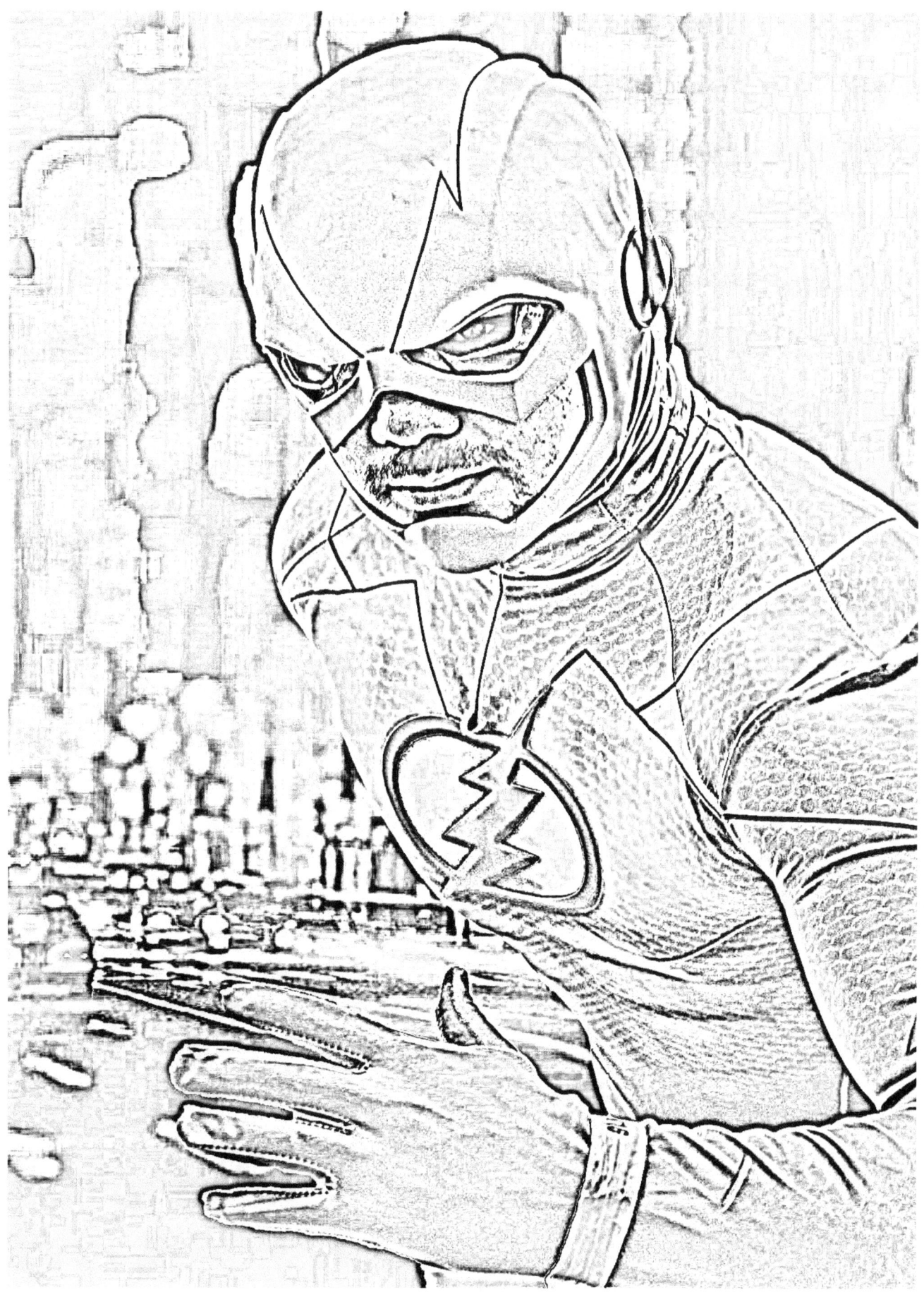

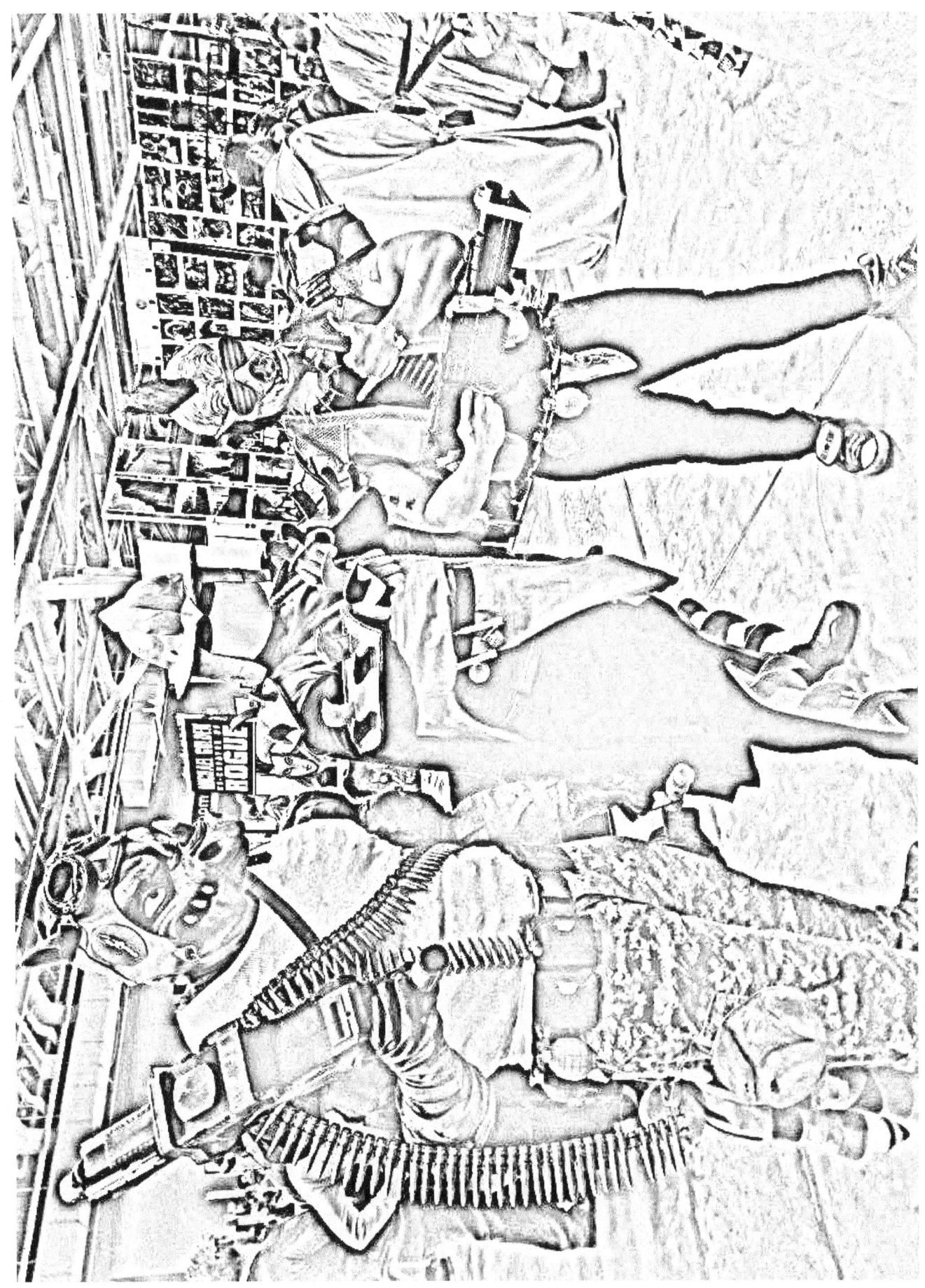

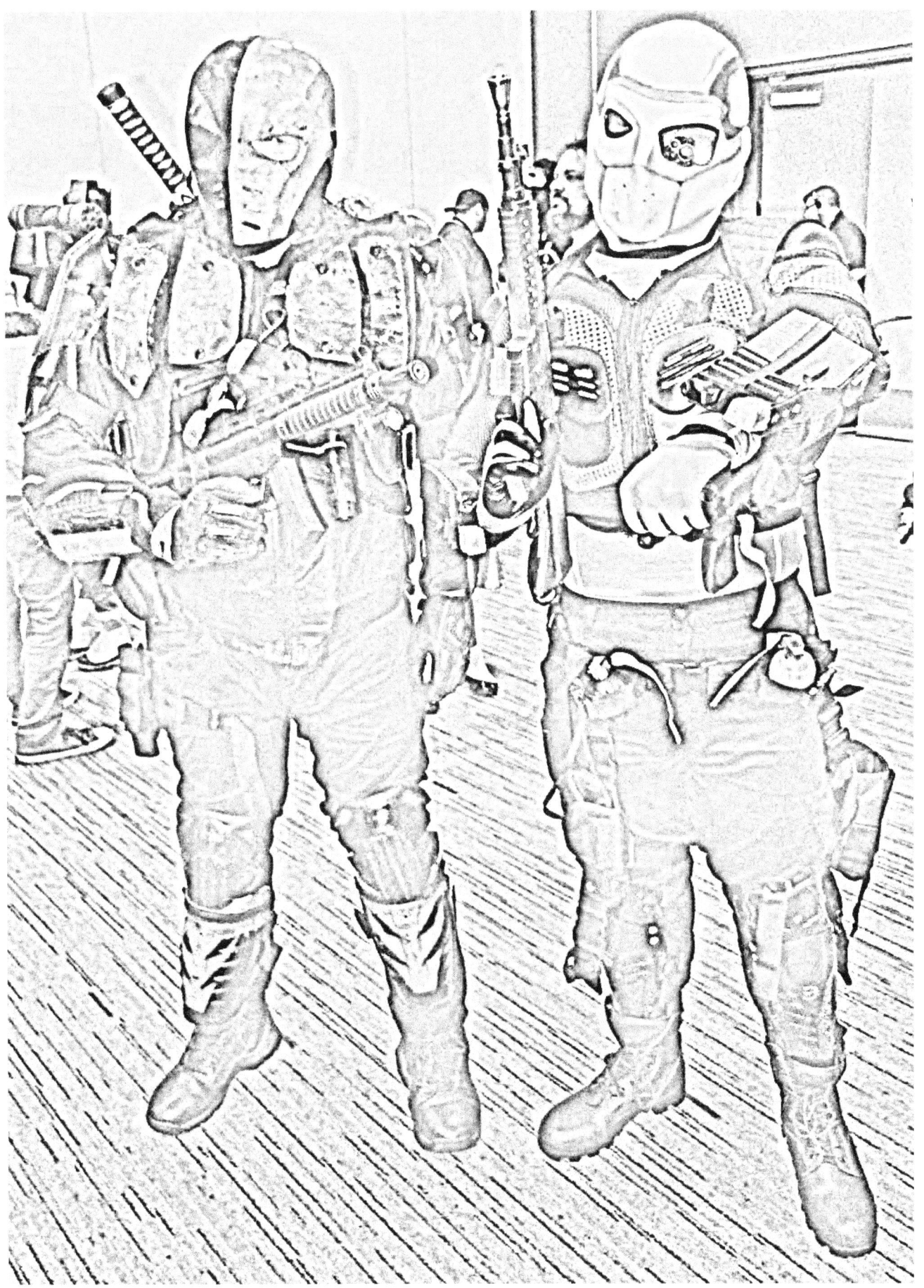

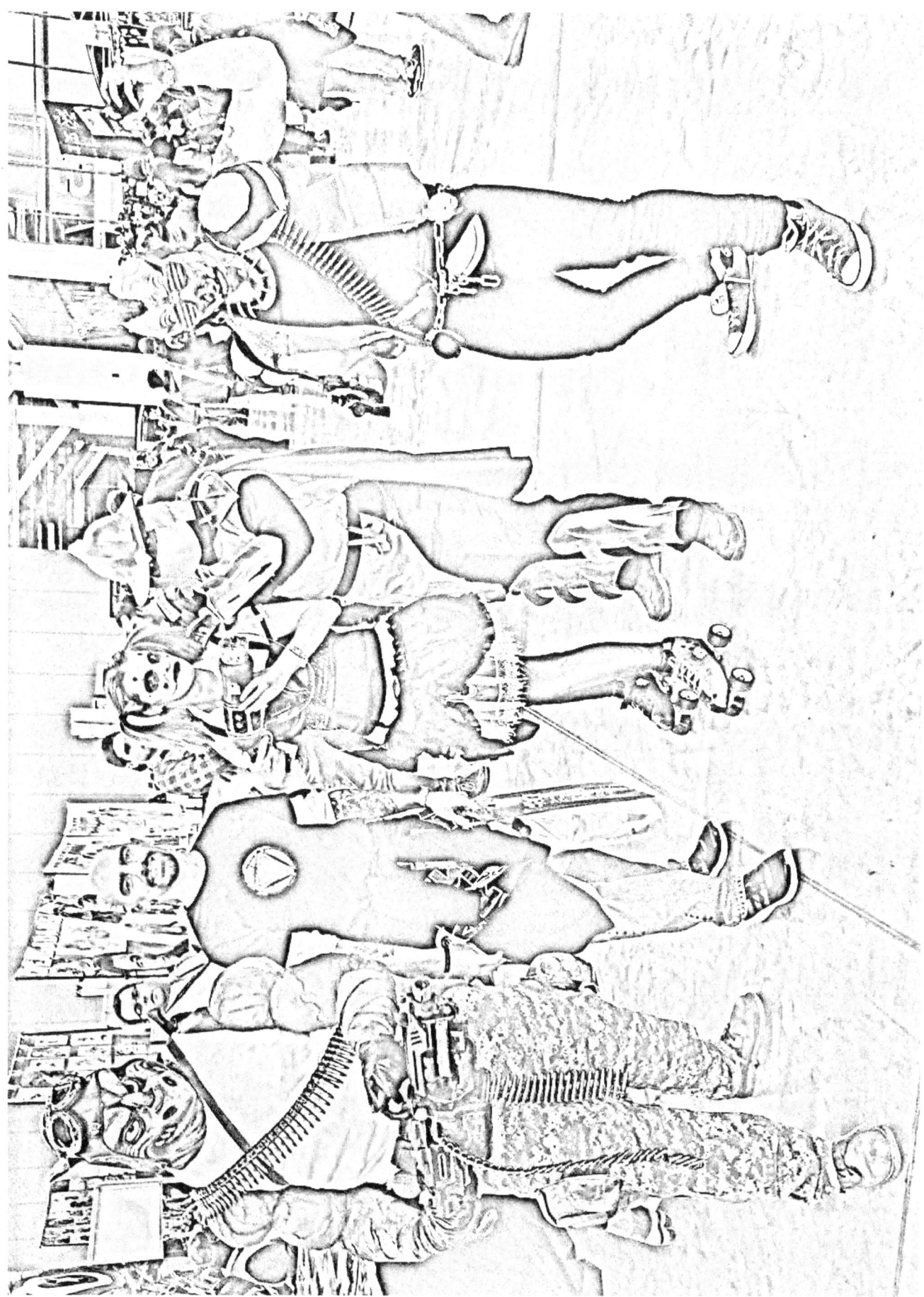

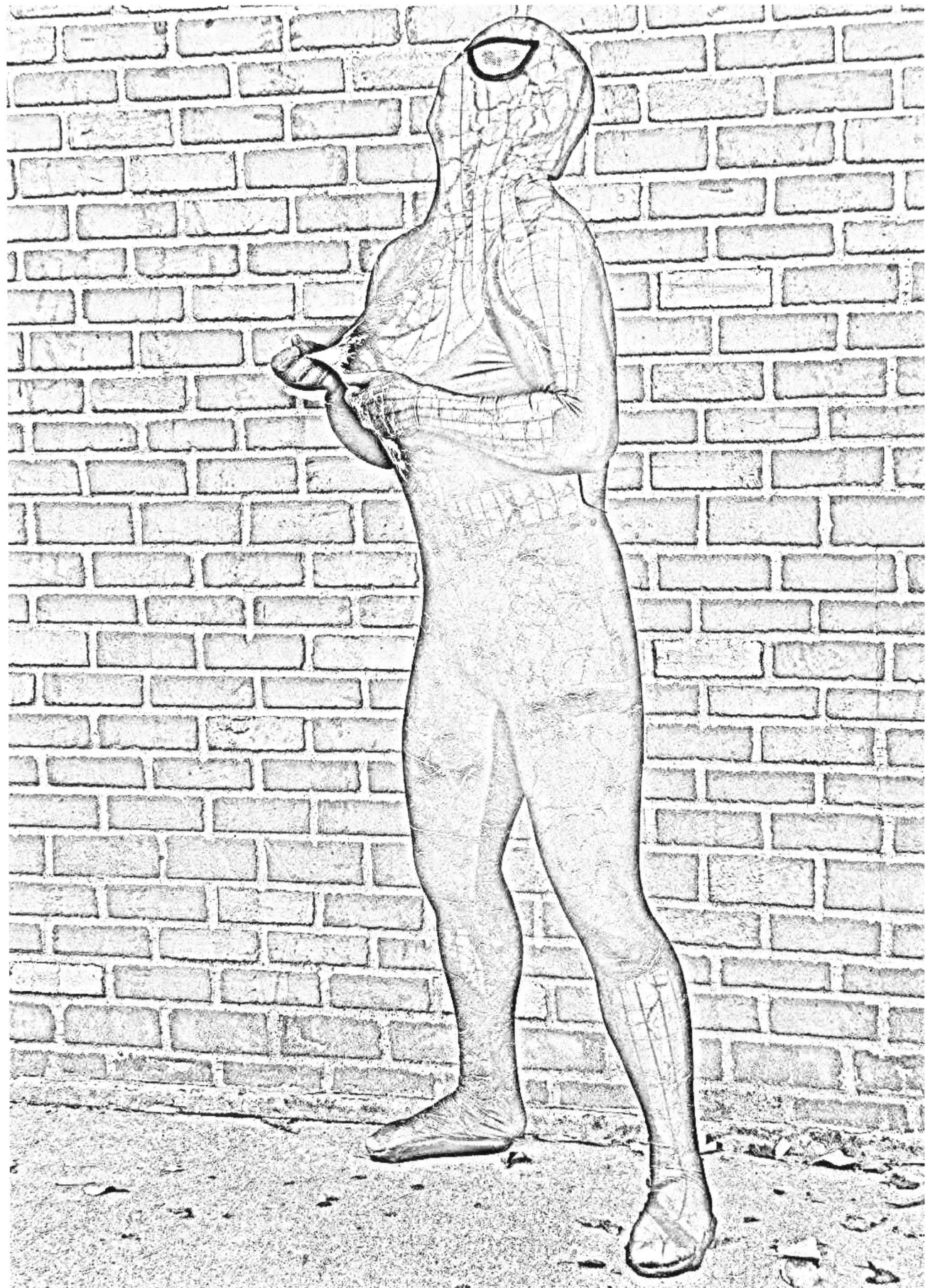

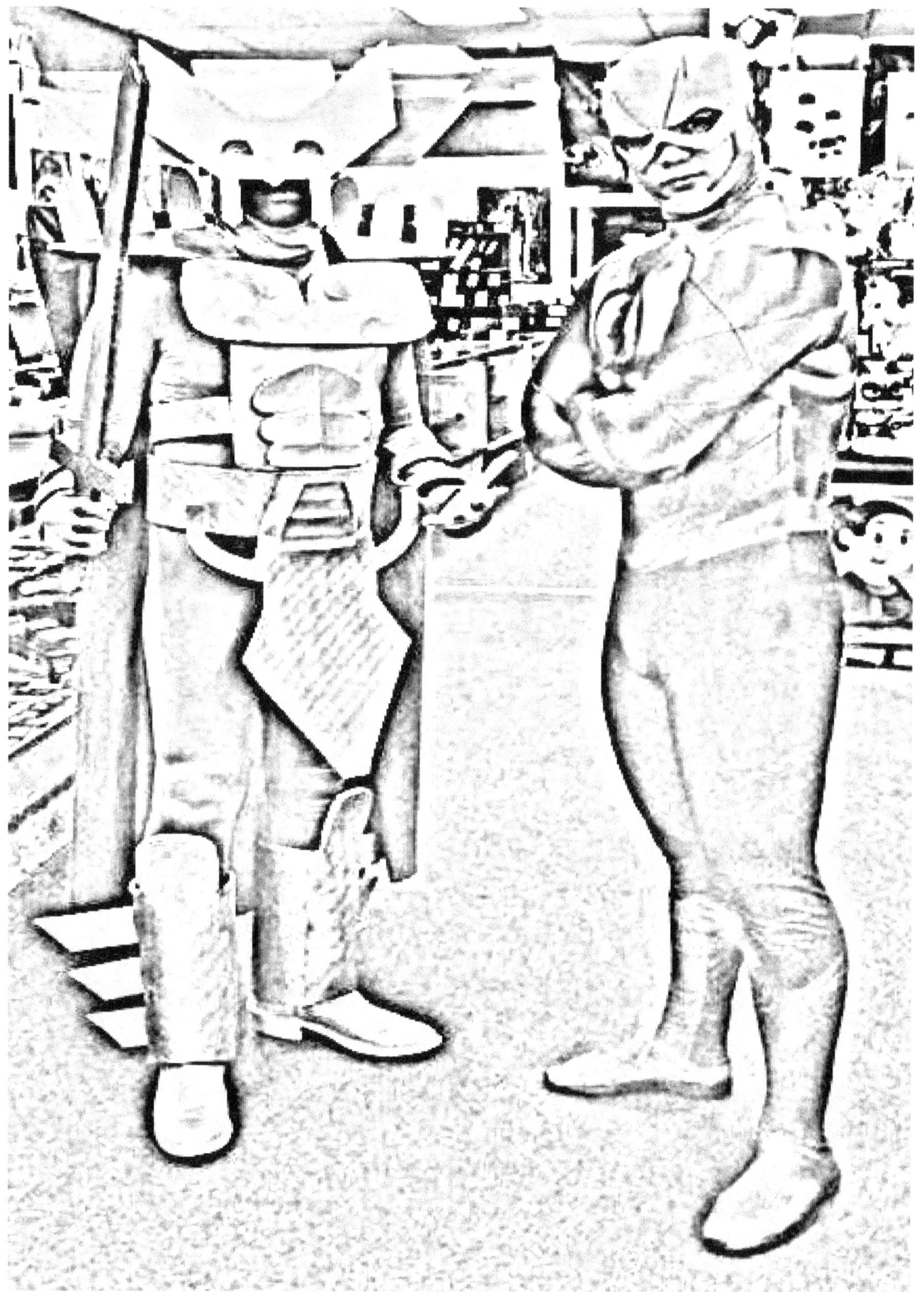

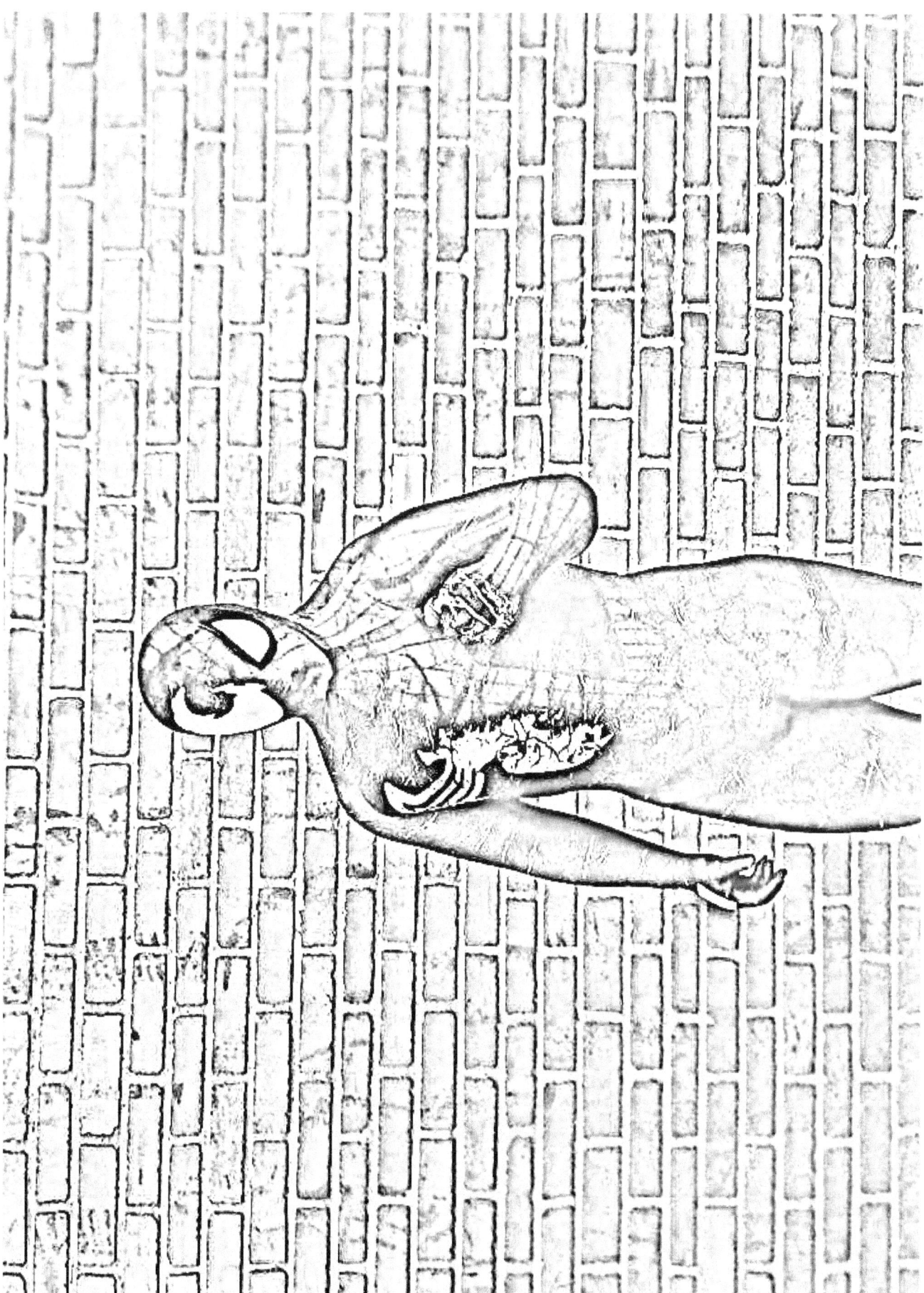

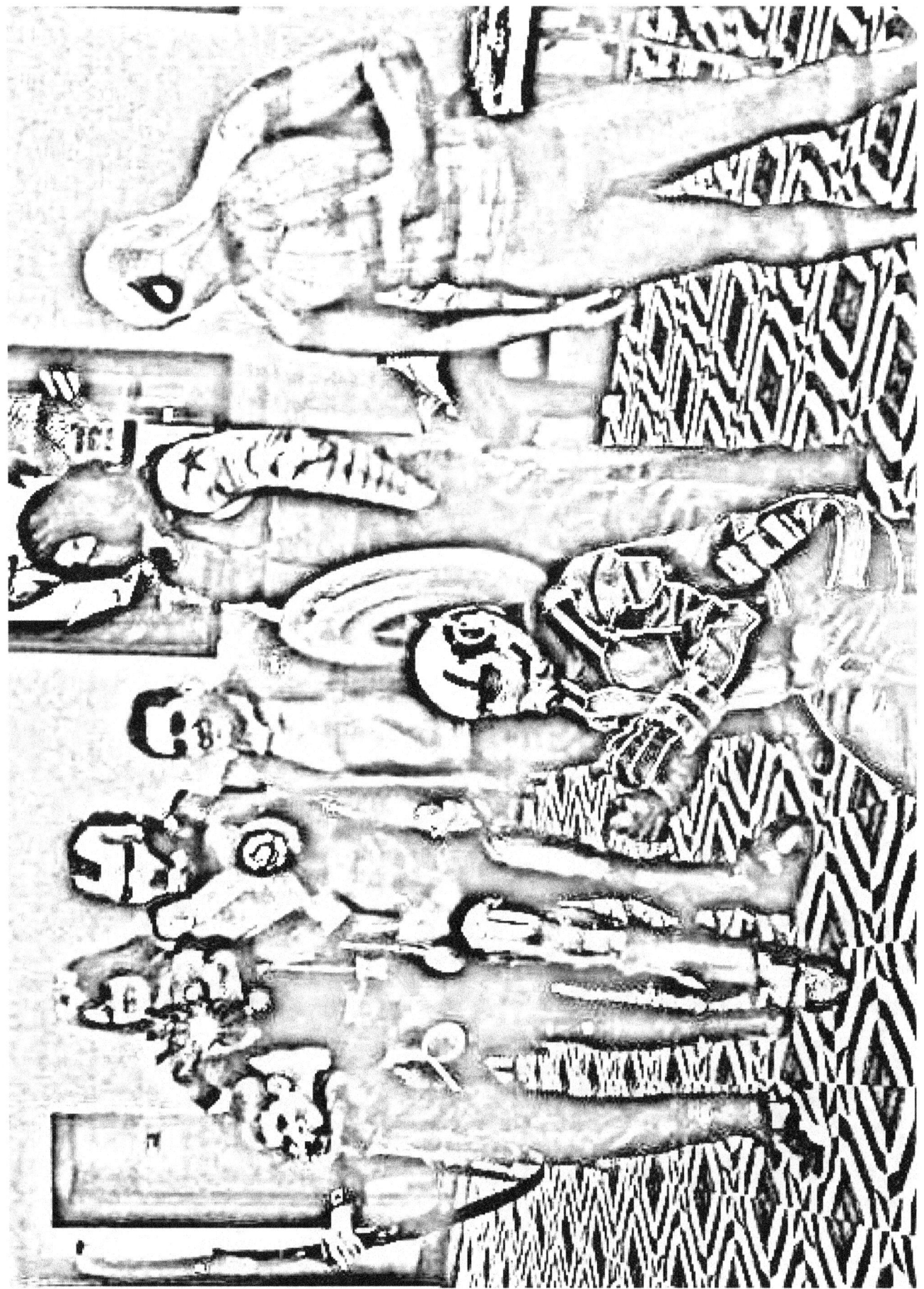

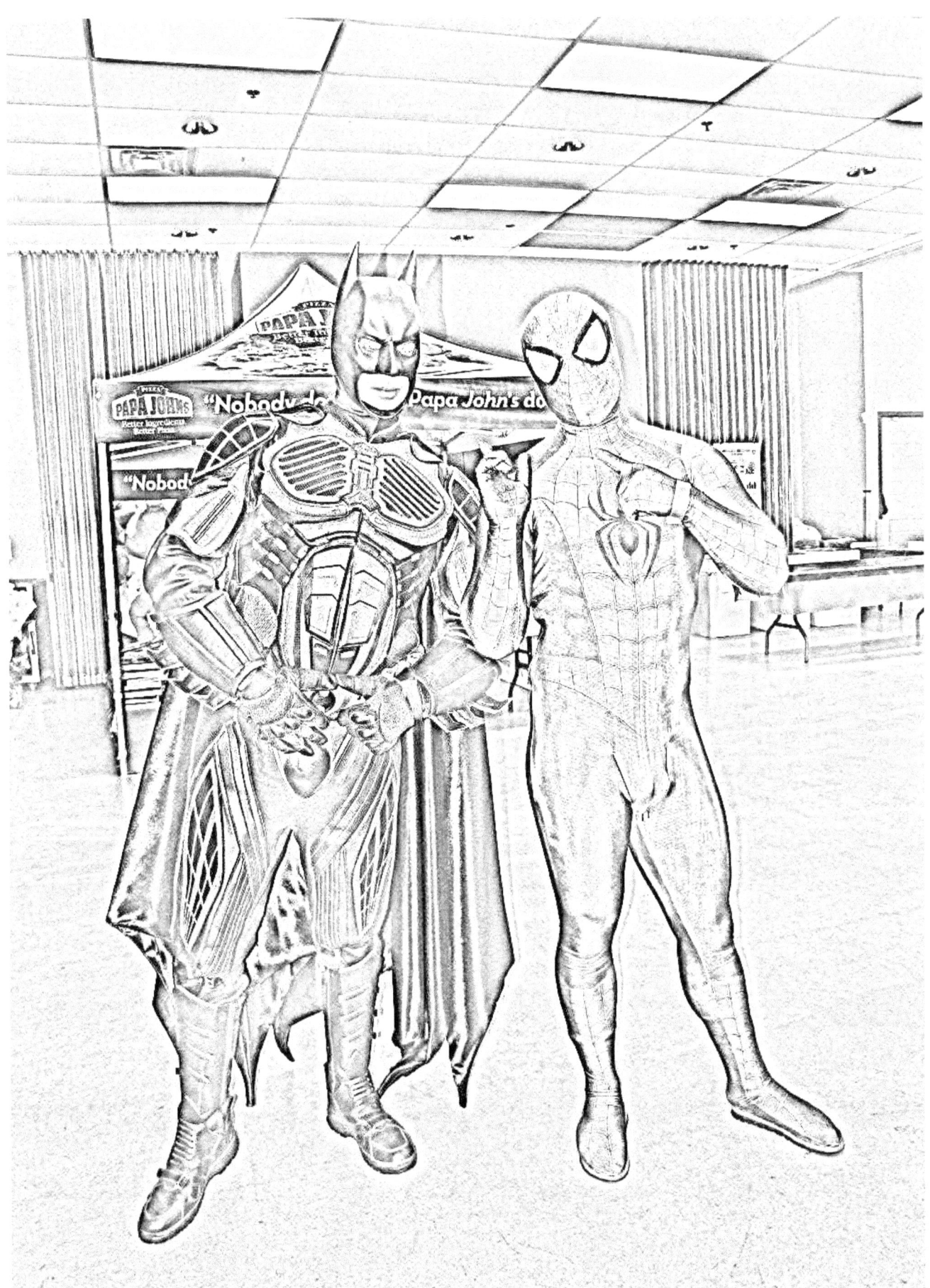

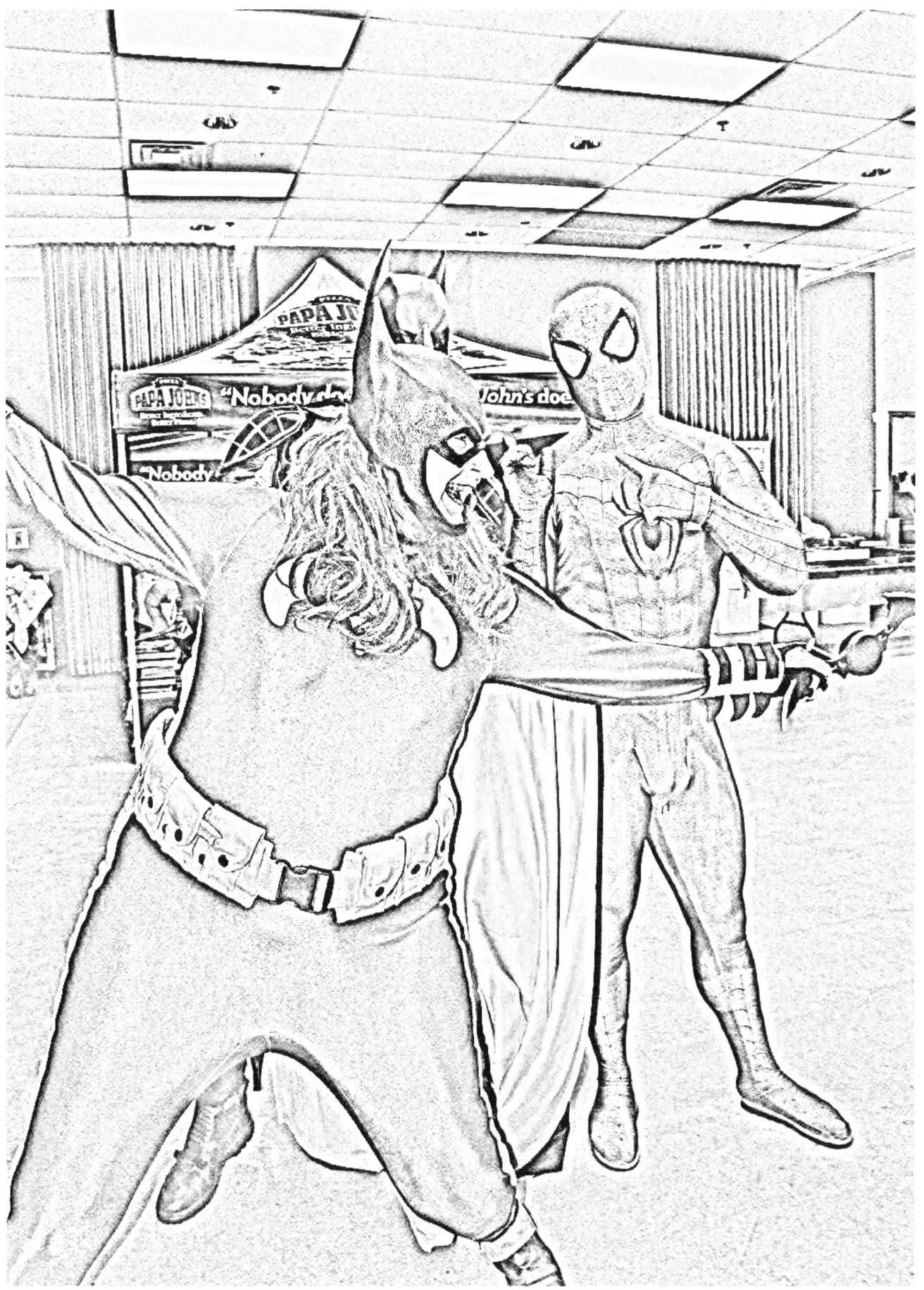

Thank You!
We hope you enjoyed our book.

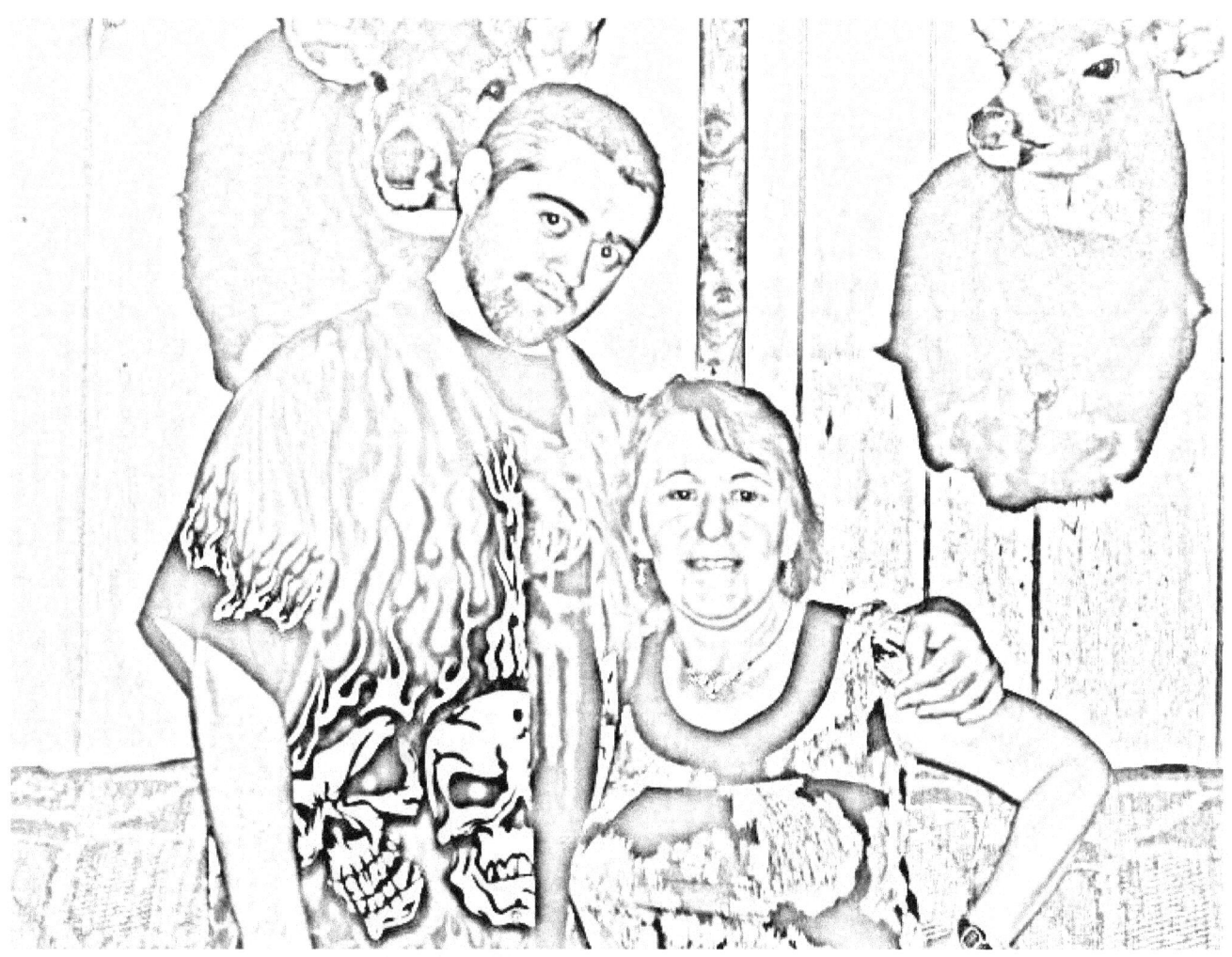

Watch for more color books by ARN Arts LLC.
Visit us at http://arnarts.wixsite.com/books

Special Thanks to Sebastian Luu for his pictures of himself & his friends at various conventions.

The pictures were found at: https://www.facebook.com/ sebastiandavidluu.

www.ingramcontent.com/pod-product-compliance
Lightning Source LLC
Chambersburg PA
CBHW081123180526
45170CB00008B/2973